THE
RENAISSANCE
AND
NEW WORLD

Giovanni Caselli

Macdonald

A MACDONALD BOOK

© Macdonald & Company (Publishers) Ltd. 1985

First published in Great Britain in 1985 by
Macdonald & Company (Publishers) Ltd.
London & Sydney

A BPCC plc company

Printed and bound by
Henri Proost
Turnhout, Belgium

Macdonald & Company (Publishers) Ltd.
Maxwell House
74 Worship Street
London EC2A 2EN

BRITISH LIBRARY CATALOGUING IN PUBLICATION DATA

Caselli, Giovanni
Renaissance and new world
I. Europe – Social life and customs
1. Title
940.2   GT129
ISBN 0-356-05976-6

Giovanni Caselli wishes to thank the
following people for their help:

Kareen Taylerson

Giuliano Fornari

Shirley Willis

David Salaryia

Editorial and research by
Jacqueline Morley

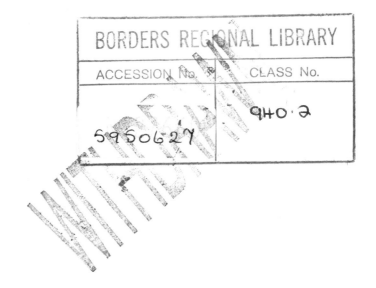

Introduction

This is the third in a series of five books which tell the story of daily life from the earliest civilizations to the modern age. This volume and its successor will concentrate on the post-medieval culture of Western Europe as it appears in the everyday objects which people used, the houses they built and the luxuries they could afford. It tells how this culture was taken across the seas to the New World, and what happened to it there.

It is plainly not possible to depict a 'typical' Renaissance or eighteenth-century person in the same sense that one can portray a typical Iron Age farmer or Viking colonist. This book therefore illustrates a selection of people whose ways of life throw light on the society that was developing around them. It also looks beyond England to wherever, in other parts of Europe, people were engaged in new activities, discovering new processes or inventing new tools which altered people's lives.

Volume two in this series closed with the evolution of the medieval town, where independent artisans made and sold their goods and country-dwellers brought small surpluses to sell. The story resumes in the fifteenth century with the rise of the international merchants whose initiative was so much a part of the Renaissance spirit. This book describes how the growth of long-distance trade and international commerce, the coming of new technology and the discovery of new worlds affected the lives of ordinary people up to the eve of the Industrial Revolution. This is a further chapter in the story of men and women as users of tools and makers of objects, but one in which the individual's identity is now established not so much by what they can make as by what they can afford to buy.

Contents

Italy: the Merchant of Prato

As populations grew in the later Middle Ages, trade expanded. Enterprising men were able to make great fortunes. A new middle class of prosperous merchants grew up in the towns. Italy at that time was perhaps the most civilized country in Europe and its merchants were regarded as the most enterprising. They brought luxuries from the east to sell to the countries of northern Europe and then carried back wool, timber, wheat and hides to the south.

An international trader no longer travelled with his goods, as in the days of Marco Polo; he sent them by sea carrier to his agents in the major European ports. Instead of paying for goods abroad by transporting real coins, the Italians devised the 'bill of exchange', a note authorizing payment at an office in one country from money received in another. They also invented double-entry book keeping to record such transactions. By making trade easier and accounting more accurate, these methods laid the foundations of modern commerce.

The merchant of Prato

Some Italian merchant families became enormously rich and powerful; they lent money to the kings of Europe and were patrons of the great Renaissance artists. Though his fortune was more modest, a certain merchant of Prato, near Florence, is especially remembered. When he died in 1410 he left his house, containing all his letters and business papers, to his native town. They survive today to show exactly how he lived.

Francesco di Marco Datini was a poor inn-keeper's son who set off to France to make his fortune in Avignon, at that time a great international trading centre. Francesco traded in armour and luxury goods: spices, Italian linen and pictures, French enamelled jewellery. Soon he had two flourishing import and export companies and three shops. In rich and respected middle age he came home to Prato with his young bride Margherita.

The new house

In Prato, Francesco built a fine new house which was the wonder of the town. Built of plastered brick, with painted decorations inside and out, it had an enclosed courtyard with a well – great luxuries where town land was limited and most families fetched their water from public fountains. In the latest fashion, the house had a loggia – an open colonnaded area for entertaining – on each floor; the upper one served also for drying clothes.

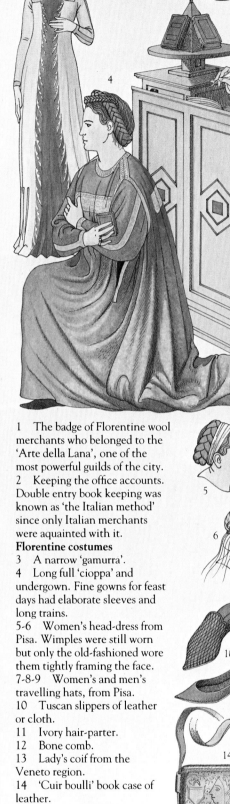

1 The badge of Florentine wool merchants who belonged to the 'Arte della Lana', one of the most powerful guilds of the city.
2 Keeping the office accounts. Double entry book keeping was known as 'the Italian method' since only Italian merchants were aquainted with it.
Florentine costumes
3 A narrow 'gamurra'.
4 Long full 'cioppa' and undergown. Fine gowns for feast days had elaborate sleeves and long trains.
5-6 Women's head-dress from Pisa. Wimples were still worn but only the old-fashioned wore them tightly framing the face.
7-8-9 Women's and men's travelling hats, from Pisa.
10 Tuscan slippers of leather or cloth.
11 Ivory hair-parter.
12 Bone comb.
13 Lady's coif from the Veneto region.
14 'Cuir boulli' book case of leather.
15 Venetian gold ear-ring.
16 Venetian silver bow-ring, worn in the East upon the thumb, for releasing the bow string.
17 Venetian brooch.
18 Venetian belt hook.
19 Iron buttons from Impruneta, Florence.

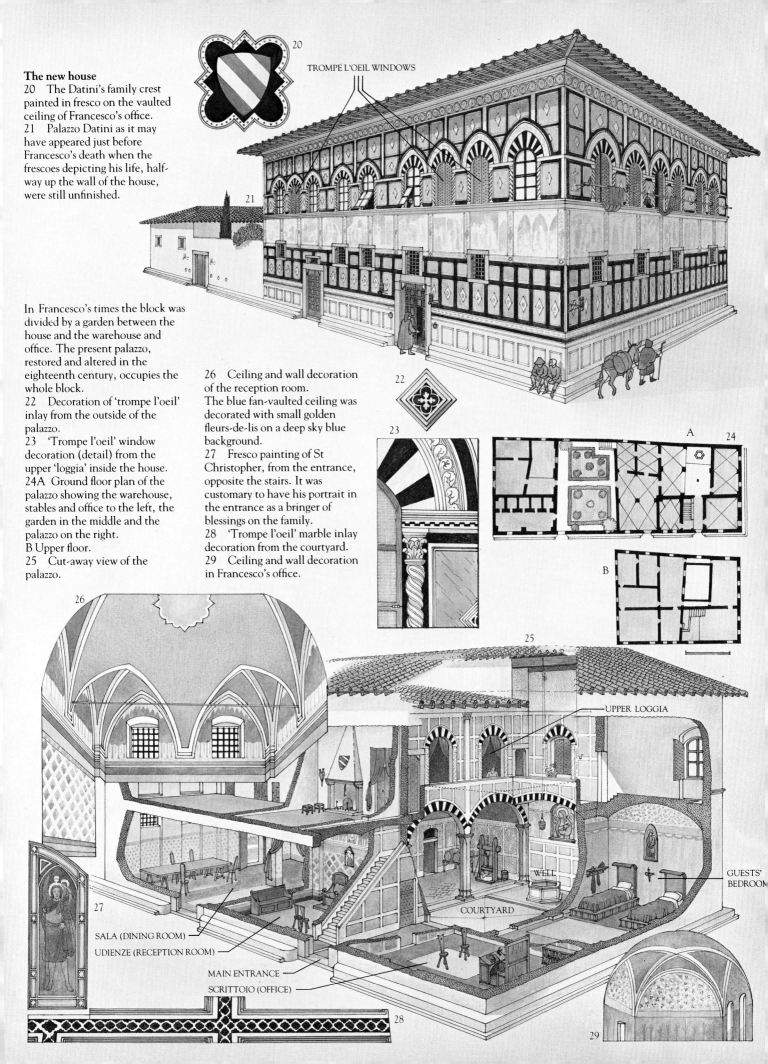

The new house
20   The Datini's family crest painted in fresco on the vaulted ceiling of Francesco's office.
21   Palazzo Datini as it may have appeared just before Francesco's death when the frescoes depicting his life, half-way up the wall of the house, were still unfinished.

In Francesco's times the block was divided by a garden between the house and the warehouse and office. The present palazzo, restored and altered in the eighteenth century, occupies the whole block.
22   Decoration of 'trompe l'oeil' inlay from the outside of the palazzo.
23   'Trompe l'oeil' window decoration (detail) from the upper 'loggia' inside the house.
24A Ground floor plan of the palazzo showing the warehouse, stables and office to the left, the garden in the middle and the palazzo on the right.
B Upper floor.
25   Cut-away view of the palazzo.

26   Ceiling and wall decoration of the reception room. The blue fan-vaulted ceiling was decorated with small golden fleurs-de-lis on a deep sky blue background.
27   Fresco painting of St Christopher, from the entrance, opposite the stairs. It was customary to have his portrait in the entrance as a bringer of blessings on the family.
28   'Trompe l'oeil' marble inlay decoration from the courtyard.
29   Ceiling and wall decoration in Francesco's office.

20

TROMPE L'OEIL WINDOWS

21

22

23

A   24

B

25

UPPER LOGGIA

WELL

GUESTS' BEDROOM

COURTYARD

27

SALA (DINING ROOM)

UDIENZE (RECEPTION ROOM)

MAIN ENTRANCE

SCRITTOIO (OFFICE)

28

29

Behind the house lay a pleasure garden and a warehouse containing Francesco's main office. Furniture was sparse. Most important was the bed, surrounded by a low footboard which served both as bench and storage chest. Other chests and small coffers held linen, fur and jewels. At the bed head hung a 'capoletto' or canopy of cloth; curtains of wool or painted linen were drawn round to make a little room. The brick floors were polished and waxed. A great deal was spent on clothes for it was important to cut a fine figure.

Margherita's work

Margherita worked hard. She superintended the milling of flour and baking of loaves, the care of the oil jars and wine barrels, the salting and preserving. She was responsible for the kitchen garden and the stables. Almost daily she prepared home produce to be carried by mule to her husband in Florence, where he lived on business, and counted and stored the town delicacies he sent to Prato. Many letters passed between them. In one Francesco lists the linen he is sending home to be washed, together with thirty herrings and a sack of capers. He asks for '. . . a jar of dried raisins, fifty oranges, bread and a barrel of vinegar . . . remember to wash the mules feet in hot water . . . have my hose made and soled. Give some millet to the nag and see it is well washed . . .' He never ceased to supervise and find fault. Margherita had three or four servants and several slaves to help her. The importation of slaves, mostly Tartars from the Black Sea area, was officially allowed provided they were not Christians; by 1400 most well-to-do Tuscan households had at least one.

From merchant to landowner

Prato was a cloth-making town. Local wool produced only poor cloth; Francesco's wealth and foreign contacts enabled him to import fine wool from England and Spain and to sell his cloth abroad. The complete process from ordering raw wool to selling finished cloth could take up to three and a half years. His accounts show that his net profit on cloth-making was under 9%. His real fortune was made in luxury goods and spices.

Like many newly-rich merchants Francesco wanted to become a landowner. A few miles from Prato he bought farmland where he built a villa and houses for the farm workers. The farm produced wheat, wine, olives and fresh produce for the Prato household. Gradually he bought up other plots until he owned 300 acres of orchards and farms. Many were let to tenants who paid rent in kind; some were worked according to the *mezzadria* system: the landowner supplied the farm and equipment and the peasant the labour; they shared the profit equally.

1   The Datini's bedroom:
A   Hanging fixture for oil lamps.
B   Wooden commode.
C   Ewer and basin for washing.
D   Painted storage chest.
E   'Cappellinaio'; a hat and coat rack.
2   Costume of a female servant (from Giotto).
3   Costume of a male servant (from Giovanni da Milano). A male servant earned 25-30 florins a year, a female 10-12 florins. A slave cost 50-80 florins to buy.

Fine glass and pottery
4   Fork, knife, spoon. The table fork was a new implement; Francesco had twelve silver forks which were kept locked away.
5   Salt, oil and vinegar containers for dressing.
6   Wine bottle and plain glass.
7   A glass from Sicily.
8   A glass from Sicily (from a painting).
9   Wine jug (from a painting by Giotto). Wine was not drunk straight but always watered. This jug may have served the purpose of mixing wine with water.
10   Florentine drug jar.
11   Another drug jar, of Umbrian manufacture.
12   Jug from Viterbo.
13,14   Enamelled terracotta plates made in Tuscany.
15   Florentine jug.

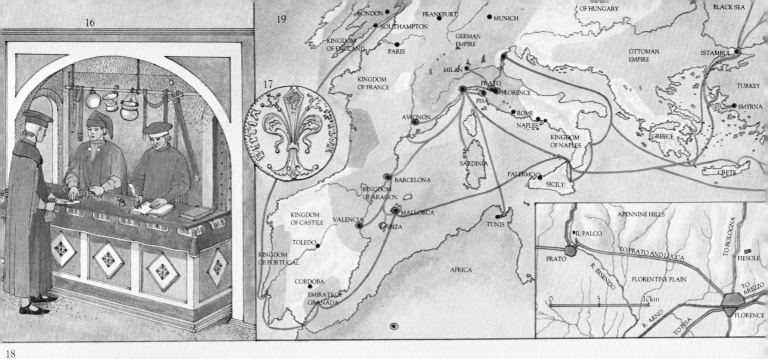

Markets and money

16 A money changer's shop in Prato, as painted by Nicola di Pietro Gerini in Datini's time. Francesco owned such a shop in Avignon.

17 The Florentine gold florin, first coined in 1252, was in use until the mid-fifteenth century. It was internationally accepted.

18 A view of the clothes market at Prato.

19 **Datini's world of trade**: Blue lines show Genoese trade routes, red lines show Venetian trade routes by sea. Red lines on land show Datini's trade routes. Tinted areas show political divisions in Europe at the close of the fourteenth century.

▽ **The country house**
Il Palco: Datini's country house and farm. The house with its garden and park stands at the western edge of a gentle slope cultivated with vineyards, olive and other fruit trees, wheat and legumes. The land was divided into smallholdings, each with its peasant dwelling at the centre.
20A A scratch plough and a plough-share as they still exist in the valley north of Prato. The plough at this time might have been smaller than at present.
20B-C-D Mattock, foot-rest spade and two pronged hoe.
E   Pruning billhook.
F   Olive-picking basket.
G   Harvesting sickle.
H   The Tuscan bushel.
21   Peasant costume from paintings by Giovanni da Milano and Giotto. Peasants used to wear short tunics of coarse homespun, called 'bigella'.

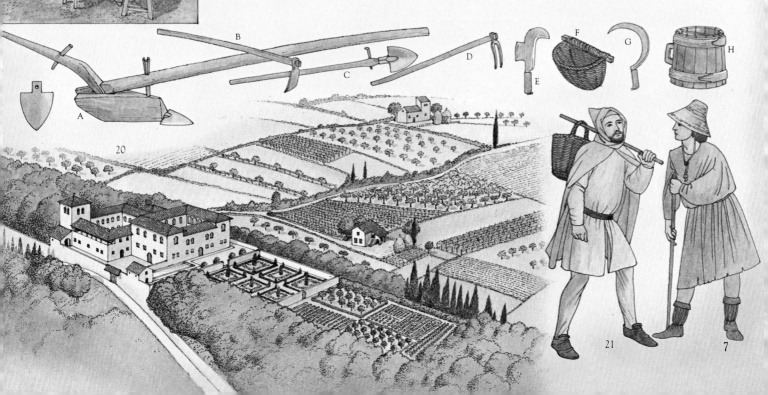

7

The Manorial Estate in Transition

The English manor house of the fifteenth century was more comfortable and convenient than its predecessors. The arrangement of its rooms also reflected a changing way of life. The strength of a feudal overlord had formerly depended on the loyalty of his men whom, in return, he had protected against a hostile world. With the slackening of feudal ties this sense of solidarity had been lost. Except on great feast days the lord no longer lived and dined with his household, but withdrew, with his family, to private apartments.

Cothay Manor

Cothay Manor, in Somerset, clearly shows how an up-to-date country house of the time was planned. The large upper chamber, or solar, for the lord's use is reached by a private staircase from his parlour-dining room. The hall is no longer the largest room; it continued to decline in importance through the centuries until, in today's house, it is merely the entrance lobby. Cothay's hall had a fashionable minstrel's gallery. This also provided space for the servants to join in services in the chapel. A licence for a private chapel was granted by the bishop if a house was far from the parish church.

The main building was approached through a gatehouse leading into the forecourt, round which were stables, storehouses and barns. Ample storage space was essential; everything that was not home produced had to be ordered in large quantities many months in advance. A working courtyard at the rear contained the brewhouse, bakehouse, dairy and laundry. The moat was now more for show than for defence, though it also provided fish for the table, drink for the horses and drainage for the lavatories.

Comfort and luxury

Life indoors was becoming more comfortable. Wealthy people now had window glass, though this was a great luxury. Walls were hung with painted cloths for warmth; the very rich had wooden panelling, or tapestry, called Arras after the Burgundian town where much of it was made. Furniture and clothes were influenced by the elegant courts of France and Burgundy. Fashions were very exaggerated. Young men wore very short jackets over even shorter doublets, and a variety of hats. Hose cut on the cross reached almost to the waist, like tights. Excessively pointed shoes were stuffed with tow or hay. Women wore a variety of fantastic head-dresses, though never so extreme in England as in France, where entrances had to be altered for them.

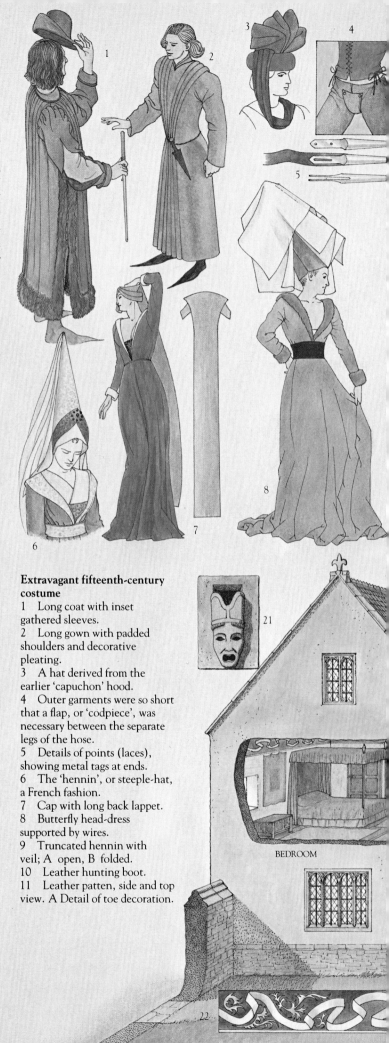

Extravagant fifteenth-century costume
1   Long coat with inset gathered sleeves.
2   Long gown with padded shoulders and decorative pleating.
3   A hat derived from the earlier 'capuchon' hood.
4   Outer garments were so short that a flap, or 'codpiece', was necessary between the separate legs of the hose.
5   Details of points (laces), showing metal tags at ends.
6   The 'hennin', or steeple-hat, a French fashion.
7   Cap with long back lappet.
8   Butterfly head-dress supported by wires.
9   Truncated hennin with veil; A open, B folded.
10   Leather hunting boot.
11   Leather patten, side and top view. A Detail of toe decoration.

BEDROOM

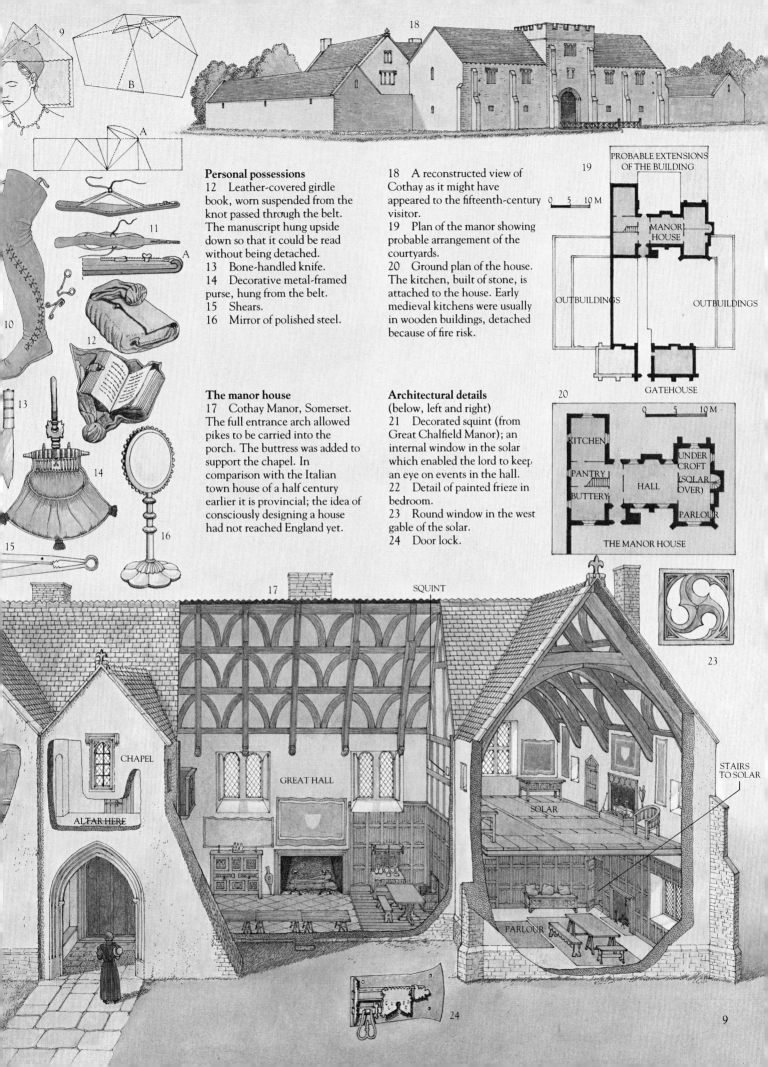

Personal possessions

12   Leather-covered girdle book, worn suspended from the knot passed through the belt. The manuscript hung upside down so that it could be read without being detached.
13   Bone-handled knife.
14   Decorative metal-framed purse, hung from the belt.
15   Shears.
16   Mirror of polished steel.

The manor house

17   Cothay Manor, Somerset. The full entrance arch allowed pikes to be carried into the porch. The buttress was added to support the chapel. In comparison with the Italian town house of a half century earlier it is provincial; the idea of consciously designing a house had not reached England yet.

18   A reconstructed view of Cothay as it might have appeared to the fifteenth-century visitor.
19   Plan of the manor showing probable arrangement of the courtyards.
20   Ground plan of the house. The kitchen, built of stone, is attached to the house. Early medieval kitchens were usually in wooden buildings, detached because of fire risk.

Architectural details
(below, left and right)
21   Decorated squint (from Great Chalfield Manor); an internal window in the solar which enabled the lord to keep an eye on events in the hall.
22   Detail of painted frieze in bedroom.
23   Round window in the west gable of the solar.
24   Door lock.

19   PROBABLE EXTENSIONS OF THE BUILDING

0   5   10 M

MANOR HOUSE

OUTBUILDINGS   OUTBUILDINGS

GATEHOUSE

20

0   5   10 M

KITCHEN

PANTRY

BUTTERY

HALL

UNDER CROFT (SOLAR OVER)

PARLOUR

THE MANOR HOUSE

17

SQUINT

CHAPEL

ALTAR HERE

GREAT HALL

SOLAR

STAIRS TO SOLAR

PARLOUR

23

24

9

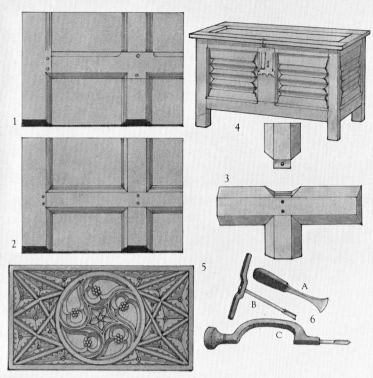

The technique of panelled furniture construction also came from the continent, probably originating in Italy. It enabled lighter and more elegant pieces to be made. Chests with 'linen-fold' panelling were imported from Flanders, and later made in England. A buffet was essential in great households, to display the gold and silver vessels which proclaimed their owner's wealth. This was a tier of open shelves for ornamental cups and plates, hence its English name of 'cupboard'.

Changes on the manorial estate

The manorial estate was also changing. Tools and practices had altered little since Norman times; the spade might now have an entirely metal blade, for iron was more readily available, but the plough and harrow remained the farmer's most elaborate implements. The real change was in the use and appearance of the land. In many places large open fields of strip-crops had given way to smaller enclosed pastures. This change reflected the fading of feudal obligations; many serfs had saved up to buy their freedom and, increasingly, the villein's duty to work on the lord's land had been altered to a payment of rent in money or in kind. This was originally to the lord's advantage; his lands were better tilled by hired labourers than by peasants who grudgingly left their own strips on certain days. But the acute shortage of labour created by the Black Death caused wages to rise sharply. Many lords could no longer afford to hire workers. They let their land to tenant farmers or turned the demesne to sheep farming which needed fewer men. Walls or hedges to confine the sheep appeared.

Sheep and enclosures

From 1450 onwards, growth in the demand for wool made sheep farming even more attractive. Those landlords who had absolute ownership were able to evict tenants and enclose the open fields. In many places, the peasants' strips began to disappear under grass, and sheep filled the countryside. Foreign visitors were amazed by their number. By 1500 there were three sheep for every human being in England.

The new hedged fields were not all the work of greedy landlords. Thrifty peasants had been accumulating blocks of land by buying additional strips from poorer peasants, or by exchanging with their neighbours. Then they hedged and ditched their property. A man who owned eighty or so acres could cultivate them using the labour of his family, and produce enough for his support and a surplus to sell in the town. He could afford to build a fine timber farmstead, with a hall and a parlour. The English countryside was soon scattered with the prosperous farmsteads of these new independent yeoman farmers.

△ **Joinery of the late fifteenth century**
Panels of thin wood were framed by stouter members.
1 Old fashioned joinery with mason's mitre (mitre and joint do not coincide).
2 Joiner's mitre.
3 Joint, dissociated to show shape.
4 Late fifteenth-century English oak coffer.
5 Carved wooden panel, c.1500.
6 Carpenter's tools: A chisel; B auger; C brace. The auger and the brace appeared during the fifteenth century in northern Europe.
7 Glass for windows was spun as shown in A, B, C, and then cut into panes. The small panes were leaded together.

▽ **Pottery and cooking utensils**
8 English glazed earthenware watering pot. The pot was immersed in water till full, the thumb being placed over a hole at the top. When the thumb was lifted, water sprinkled from holes in the bottom.
9 Earthenware pipkin supported on iron brandreth.
10 Chafing-dish of copper alloy to hold burning charcoal. A dish (containing food) was set on top.
11 Chimney crane and cooking pot. The kitchen fire was no longer in the centre of the room, but in a wall fireplace, making it possible to suspend cooking pots from the chimney.
12 Baluster jugs, Oxford.
13 Carinated jug, Oxford.
14 Bung hole pitcher, Cheam.
15 Bung hole pitcher, London.
16 Costrel, Winchester.

17

B

Stained glass
17 A, B, C, D. At the four corners of the page four of a series of six stained glass roundels, originally in Cassiobury Park, now in the Victoria and Albert Museum. They show the 'Labours of the Months'.

18 Sheep shearing, from a woodcut representing the month of June from *The Shepherd's Great Calendar*, printed at the end of the fifteenth century.

Houses and fields
19 Typical house of a prosperous yeoman farmer. Wealden house with recessed front at Daniel's Water, Kent.

20 Transition from sub-divided fields based on strips, top right, through intermixed blocks and parcels, bottom right, to enclosed fields, bottom left. Based on a plan of Little Rollright, Oxfordshire, in the fifteenth century.

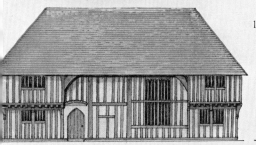

19

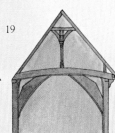

20

Farming equipment
21 Hedger's tools: billhook and staking mallet.
22 The hedge:
A a ditch is dug and soil thrown over nearby bush.
B the bush grows up through the soil; the lower growth is trimmed.
C the bush crowns the bank. A hedgerow is formed by layering and trimming the bushes.
23 Fifteenth-century spades; iron shod wooden spades.
24 All-metal spade which re-appeared in the fifteenth century, having been absent from Britain since Roman times when it was common.
25 A bushel measure for corn. It was levelled off with a stick.
26 Winnowing fan, brought by the Romans. Grain was tossed up in it, and the air current blew the light chaff away.
27 Southern English plough as it probably was from the fifteenth century. It was attached to a wheel-carriage.

18

21

22 A B C

23

26

25

24

28 English farm cart, before the introduction of the four-wheeled waggon into Britain from the Low Countries in the sixteenth century.
29 Shepherd's crook.
30 Kidney-shaped seed basket for broadcast sowing.

C

27

28

29

30

D

11

Nuremberg: Renaissance Technology

Until the recent inventions of telephone and broadcasting, ideas, like objects, could only move about if they were carried, either by word of mouth or in books. For this reason, Southern Germany was one of the first regions outside Italy to receive the new ideas which so excited Italian artists and scholars in the fifteenth century. The great trade route from Italy to the Low Countries carried new ideas to Nuremberg, a rich commercial city renowned for its skilled metal working. Its craftsmen excelled as armourers, goldsmiths, silversmiths and jewellers. Such skills proved to be of practical value to many Renaissance scholars. Stimulated by the rediscovery of Greek mathematics, they sought to establish the exact nature of the universe by astronomical observations. This created an intense demand for delicate scientific instruments: astrolabes, armillaries and sundials.

The craftsmen of Nuremberg had all the expertise needed to make these instruments. Regiomontanus, a German astronomer and mathematician whose work influenced Copernicus, settled in Nuremberg in 1471. He chose the city because, he said, he found there 'all the peculiar instruments necessary for astronomy, and there it is easiest for me to keep in touch with the learned of all countries, for this city, on account of its concourse of merchants, may be considered the central point of Europe.'

The development of printing and new weapons

He would also have found there another of Germany's great contributions to the spread of Renaissance ideas: the printed book. Wood-block printing on textiles had been known in Europe from very early times, but until paper became freely available there was little reason to think of printing books. Paper-making, which the Arabs learned from the Chinese and brought to Europe in the twelfth century, was not widely practised until the fifteenth. It was then that the printing of text from moveable type was evolved in southern Germany. The making of metal type by precision casting required great skill. Large-scale publishing therefore first became established among the metalworkers of Nuremberg.

German metalworkers of the fifteenth century increased the amount of metal available and made better quality cast iron by using larger blast furnaces with huge water-powered bellows. Metal tools and machine parts came into use. Bronze founders, who had perfected their technique in the casting of church bells, now turned to casting cannon, and the craft of gunsmith came into being. In the next two centuries, new methods of warfare, employing guns and armed ships, turned Europe into a dominant world power.

Nuremberg metal work

22   Iron candlestick for ordinary household use.
23   Bronze fountain head.
24   Iron candlestick. The candle holder is pierced to allow the candle stub to be pushed out and the precious wax to be re-used.
25   Pewter serving flagon.
26   Forge bellows operated by water power. Trip hammers compressed the bellows and counterweights opened them again.
27   Section through a tall 'stückofen', an improved type of iron-smelting furnace developed in Germany. This type of furnace could raise sufficient heat to make cast iron, which was very important for the development of tools and fire-arms.

△   Excavating a mine. The spoil is being hauled to the surface by bucket, rope and windlass.

Miner's digging tools
15A pike; B hoe; C pick; D shovel.
16   Containers for hauling ore and spoil up the shafts. A basket; B ox-hide bucket: C wooden bucket bound with iron.
17   Miner's steel axe used for shaping the timbers which shored up the mine tunnels.
18   Miner's wheelbarrow.

Precision goods
19   Spring-driven clock.
20   Globe made at Nuremberg in 1492 by Martin Behaim, who was a pupil of Regiomontanus and passed his knowledge on to Christopher Columbus.
21   Jeweller's scales for weighing gold, tweezers, and a box of weights.

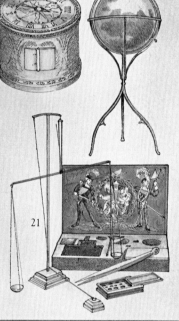

Printing
28   A printer's workshop and adjoining bookshop. The compositor sits with his copy in front of him picking up type to place in his composing stick. He will then set it in the two-page forme by his side. The full forme will be placed on the stone bed of the press where it will be inked. The paper will be placed on a hinged leaf and brought down over the type. A prepared forme, with the paper in place, is on the bed ready to be slid under the screw of the press.
29   Playing cards. The earliest printing on paper was from blocks, with pictures and text cut in one piece of wood.
30   Gothic type face.

On facing page:
1   Dürer's house, Nuremberg. The ground floor was a printer's workshop. The scientist, Regiomontanus, also lived here.
2   A birdseller.
3   A fishmonger.
4   A portable baker's oven.
5   Nuremberg street.
6   The main room of a Nuremberg house. In an alcove is a ewer, with a tap and basin below it, for washing the hands. A roller towel hangs on one side and a brush on the other. Storage chests are used as seating. Inner wooden shutters are secured over the window.
7   Map showing Nuremberg's position at the centre of Europe's overland trade routes.
8   Wooden relief showing the Nuremberg weigh-master who checked that goods were of the standard weight.
9   Stove faced with ceramic tiles to reflect the heat. Stoves were common in Central Europe where there was plentiful timber to burn.
10   Chair.
11   Wine cooler.
12   Branched iron candlestick for a grand table.
13   Study table.
14   Kitchen interior. The cooking surface is at a working height with the fire beneath it.

Nuremberg's rapid increase in prosperity is reflected in the numerous books of etiquette produced at this time, telling the newly-rich how to behave.

It also explains why Nuremberg was cleaner and better administered than many other cities. The town was divided into several quarters responsible for such matters as defence and fire fighting. Public bath houses were required to keep large vats of water mounted on carts ready for fire-fighting. The city had fourteen licensed bath houses. Personal cleanliness was considered important; 'bathing money' was a regular part of a man's wages. Some streets had been paved in stone since 1368. The city architect was in charge of paving which was laid down at public expense to within four feet of each householder's door – the rest he had to pay himself. By 1490 a public service of 'scavengers' cleaned the streets.

Private housing in Nuremberg

By 1500 nearly every family had its own house. Fifteenth-century records show that most housed no more than two to four people, together with one or two servants and an apprentice. Living quarters were on the upper floors with workshops or storage below. Work spilled over into the street; fire regulations obliged all activities causing sparks or fumes to be carried on out of doors. The humblest houses had enough bedrooms for children to sleep separately from their parents, and servants from their employers. In times of war the city became much more crowded as people poured in from the countryside to shelter behind the safety of its walls.

Nuremberg's surrounding lands guaranteed supplies of nearly all the food the townspeople needed. They ate well and abundantly. Two meat dishes a day were not exceptional. Dishes were highly seasoned, not because meat was bad – laws against selling anything not freshly killed were strict – but because people liked them like that. For fast-days the city maintained spring-fed ponds stocked with fish.

Master craftsmen at work

Gifts of money from wealthy citizens established all sorts of charitable institutions for the sick and needy. The Mendel almshouse, founded in 1388, provided free board and lodging for retired master craftsmen. A portrait of each new inmate was painted, showing him at work among the tools of his trade. These have survived to provide an invaluable record of how each craft was practised. Two masters from each craft were responsible to the city council for the testing of every object before it could be sold.

7   From a self-portrait of Dürer. His doublet is open to show a low-necked shirt which is gathered into a small frill at the neckline.

8   Two wealthy merchants. Striped hose and parti-coloured garments were popular.

Metalwork

9   Bronze key ring. It is opened by detaching the screw that links the ring to the figures that form the handle.

10   Silver-gilt bridal crown worn by a rich merchant's daughter.

11   Bunch of keys and drawstring purse suspended by a strap which hung from the girdle.

12   Wrought and chased iron double key.

13   Small iron coffer with three hinged re-inforced bands. Such coffers guarded household valuables and important documents and also a merchant's daily takings.

1   Nuremberg guilder c. 1496-1506, showing the Nuremberg eagle and the figure of St. Lawrence.

Costume

2   A peasant and his wife.

3   A fashionable young man and woman.

4   Nuremberg women dressed for going to church.

5   Young Nuremberg girl in a dance dress.

6   Lady in ball dress.

Portraits of the inmates of the Mendel almshouse

They wear the uniform of the almshouse.

14 Lantern maker.
15 Thimble maker.
16 Goldsmith.
17 Pin maker.
18 Bridle maker.
19 File maker.
20 Pewterer.
21 Nail maker.
22 Glazier.
23 Candlestick maker.
24 Locksmith.
25 Cutler.
26 Tailor.
27 Drill-maker.
28 Armour-maker.

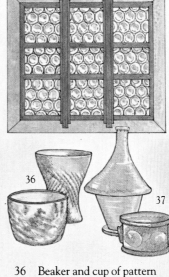

Goldsmith's work

29 Standing cup of agate mounted in silver-gilt.
30 Gold 'welcome cup'; a double cup, the upper reversed on the lower.
31 Parcel-gilt silver covered beaker.
32 Horn and silver-gilt beaker.
33 Silver-gilt box.
34 Mazer with lid, mounted in silver-gilt.

Glazier's work

35 Glazed window. The circles of glass are held together by lead strips.

36 Beaker and cup of pattern moulded glass.
37 Bottle and shallow goblet of blown glass.

Arms and armour

38 Fifteenth-century mail shirt. Every ring was made and riveted with precision.
39 Wire making. Metal, hammered into a roll, was drawn through a pierced plate.
40 The first hand guns were straight pieces of timber to which a short barrel was fastened.
41 Suit of armour made in Nuremberg.
42 Sword hilt of elaborate goldsmith's work, with bronze pommel, punched and gilded, and guard of hardened iron, etched and gilded.
43 Foreman's hammer, forged iron, etched and partly gilded.
44 Throwing-axe of forged iron.

15

England: Tudor Prosperity

In the early sixteenth century England was a small nation – there were nearly twice as many Spaniards and two and a half times as many French as English. England was comparatively unimportant in the eyes of its European neighbours. But its middle class of farmers, manufacturers and merchants was confident and resourceful; by the close of the century their practical initiative had made England a power to be reckoned with throughout the world.

A new town of the fifteenth century

From medieval times England had derived its wealth from the quality of its raw wool, which was exported all over Europe. During the fifteenth century a much larger proportion of it was woven into cloth in England. East Anglia was the chief cloth-producing region and Lavenham, in Suffolk, its most important centre. Due to changing fashion in the wool trade which robbed it of commercial importance, Lavenham has survived largely unchanged to show us what a Tudor manufacturing town was like. Originally a market town, Lavenham was largely rebuilt in the fifteenth century and reached the height of its prosperity in the early years of the sixteenth.

Timber-framed housing

At a time when most English towns had 2,000–3,000 inhabitants, Lavenham had 11,000 and was England's fourteenth-richest town. The half-timbered houses that still line every street were the substantial homes of its wealthy cloth manufacturers. Timber was still the accepted building material. Bricks were once more being made in England (the art had been lost when the Romans left) but only the grandest buildings were entirely of brick. Though Spanish visitors wondered at London's houses of 'mud and sticks', they acknowledged that there was a high standard of living inside. Even timber buildings had wall fireplaces. Brick chimneys, providing fireproof flues, were often added to the end wall of earlier buildings. They also housed internal ovens and provided hearths to warm the upper rooms.

Cloth manufacture

Many processes were involved in changing raw wool into cloth, each performed by a specialist; spinners turned the wool to yarn, dyers dyed it, weavers made the cloth, fullers steeped the loose weave and pounded it firm, shearmen raised the nap, cropped it, and straightened and pressed the finished cloth. Formerly these craftsmen had been self-employed, making their living by supplying their neighbours' needs. But during the fifteenth century, enterprising weavers realized that there were great profits to be made overseas. They

Buildings at Lavenham
1   The Hall of the Guild of Corpus Christi. The finest of Lavenham's guildhalls, completed in 1529. The guilds provided religious and social benefits for their members.
2   Linen-fold panelling in the guildhall interior, showing how it was fitted round the window.
3   Detail of the linen-fold design. A Front. B Cross section.
4   A Carved corner post of the Guildhall. B Detail of figure.
5   Master clothier's house in Church Street.
6   92 Church Street, with Tudor chimney.
7   Fifteenth-century hall of the Guild of our Lady.
8   Tudor shops, 10–11 Lady Street.
9   Houses in Water Street.
10   59-60 Water Street, originally one house, known as the De Vere House.
11   Door of the De Vere House. Large doorways for the passage of goods had smaller doors within.

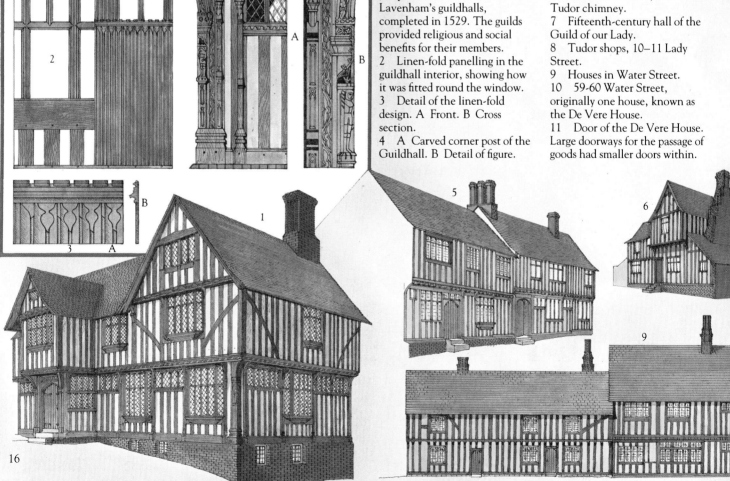

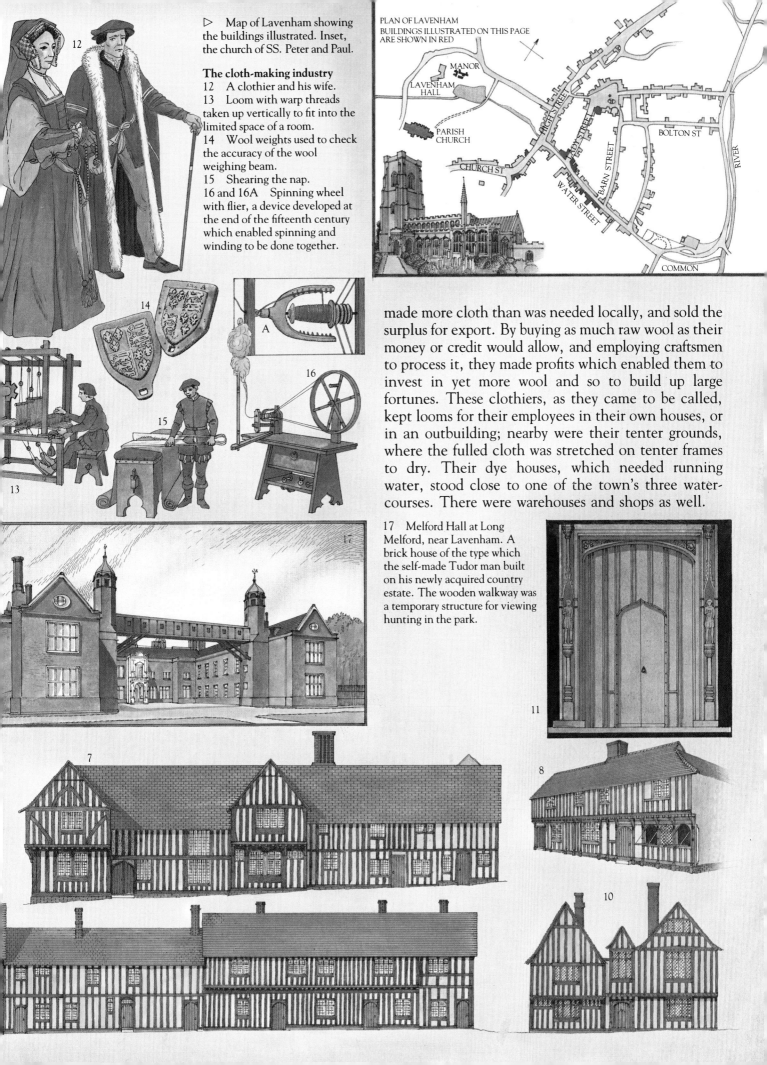

▷ Map of Lavenham showing the buildings illustrated. Inset, the church of SS. Peter and Paul.

The cloth-making industry

12 A clothier and his wife.
13 Loom with warp threads taken up vertically to fit into the limited space of a room.
14 Wool weights used to check the accuracy of the wool weighing beam.
15 Shearing the nap.
16 and 16A Spinning wheel with flier, a device developed at the end of the fifteenth century which enabled spinning and winding to be done together.

PLAN OF LAVENHAM
BUILDINGS ILLUSTRATED ON THIS PAGE ARE SHOWN IN RED

made more cloth than was needed locally, and sold the surplus for export. By buying as much raw wool as their money or credit would allow, and employing craftsmen to process it, they made profits which enabled them to invest in yet more wool and so to build up large fortunes. These clothiers, as they came to be called, kept looms for their employees in their own houses, or in an outbuilding; nearby were their tenter grounds, where the fulled cloth was stretched on tenter frames to dry. Their dye houses, which needed running water, stood close to one of the town's three water-courses. There were warehouses and shops as well.

17 Melford Hall at Long Melford, near Lavenham. A brick house of the type which the self-made Tudor man built on his newly acquired country estate. The wooden walkway was a temporary structure for viewing hunting in the park.

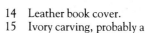

1 Tudor emblem cast on a bronze gun.
2 Sir George Carew, Vice-Admiral of the Fleet, who sank with his ship, the *Mary Rose*.
3 Dress of a nobleman.

From the *Mary Rose*.
4 Crewman's leather shoe.
5 Leather purse with gold coins. Enlarged, a gold angel coin.
6 Bosun's call, or whistle.
7 Wooden comb.
8 Bone manicure set.
9 Brass thimble.
10 Ear scoops.
11 Wooden pomander.
12 Pocket sundial, used like a modern wrist watch and about the same size.
13 A barber-surgeon. His cabin has been identified from the equipment found in it. Inset below, detail of his velvet coif as found in the wreck.

Arms and armour

Though the woollen industry declined later in the sixteenth century, other English industries were expanding. Iron working was especially important. Cannon had been known since the fourteenth century, but they were of limited use on land because they were too unwieldy to manoeuvre. At sea, however, they could be as mobile as the ships that carried them. The new aim of naval combat was therefore to shatter enemy ships with cannon shot from a distance. The best early cannon were of bronze. Though easier to cast than iron, and less liable to fracture dangerously, they were very expensive. Encouraged by Henry VII, English workers developed the technique of casting cheap but safe iron substitutes. By 1500, English ships were carrying primitive cast-iron guns, and, by the mid-century, expertise in their manufacture had given England a decisive advantage over its European rivals.

The *Mary Rose*

The raising of the carrack *Mary Rose*, lost in the English Channel in 1545, has produced a wealth of information about Tudor seafaring. The *Mary Rose* could carry 91 guns, made of brass and wrought iron. The 140 long bows found ready for use beside the archers on the upper deck prove that their skills were still highly prized. They could fire at a rate of 12–20 arrows a minute and had a range of 300 yards. The *Mary Rose* had been converted from clinker to carvel planking so that gun ports could be cut in her hull. Their use was a novelty and had not been properly mastered by her officers. Through overloading with guns and men, the *Mary Rose* began to tilt to one side. Water poured through her open gun ports and almost immediately sank her.

Tudor documents give some idea of the provisions that a warship like the *Mary Rose* would have carried. For an expedition of eight weeks the crew of 200 were provided with 5,000 kg of biscuits (about half a kilo each a day), 40,000 litres of beer (over three litres each a day), eight tonnes of 'flesh', three tonnes of fish and cheese. Bones from the *Mary Rose* show that venison, beef, pork, mutton, and chicken formed part of the 'flesh' on board. Fresh fruit and vegetables were provided; plum stones and the remains of peas still in the pod have been found. Ship's tackle, medical equipment, toilet articles, gaming boards and musical instruments all survive to show exactly what was in use on the 19 July 1545 when the ship sank.

14 Leather book cover.
15 Ivory carving, probably a book spine.
16 Table ware; pewter wine flagons and plate, spoon, candlestick, wooden drinking vessel with personal mark on lid, pepper mill and peppercorn container.

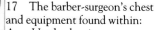

17 The barber-surgeon's chest and equipment found within:
A Urethral syringe.
B Wooden container.
C Needle.
D-F Small flasks.
G Chafing dish.
H Bronze mortar for pounding drugs.

16

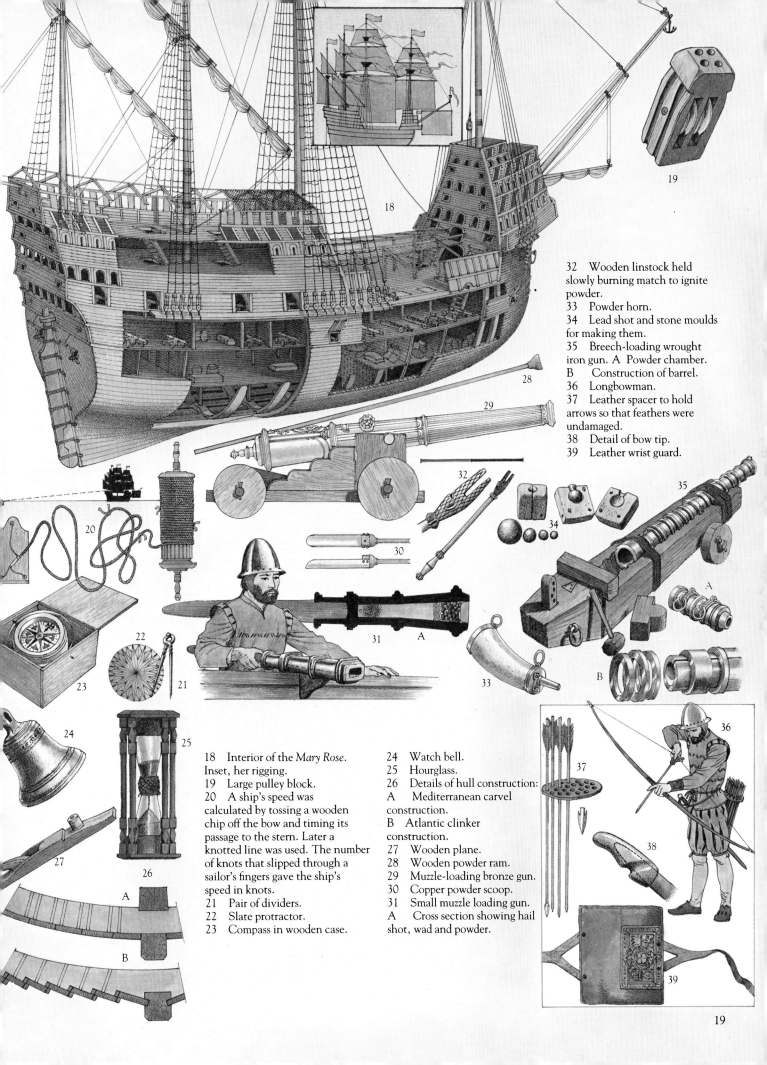

32 Wooden linstock held slowly burning match to ignite powder.
33 Powder horn.
34 Lead shot and stone moulds for making them.
35 Breech-loading wrought iron gun. A Powder chamber.
B Construction of barrel.
36 Longbowman.
37 Leather spacer to hold arrows so that feathers were undamaged.
38 Detail of bow tip.
39 Leather wrist guard.

18 Interior of the *Mary Rose*. Inset, her rigging.
19 Large pulley block.
20 A ship's speed was calculated by tossing a wooden chip off the bow and timing its passage to the stern. Later a knotted line was used. The number of knots that slipped through a sailor's fingers gave the ship's speed in knots.
21 Pair of dividers.
22 Slate protractor.
23 Compass in wooden case.

24 Watch bell.
25 Hourglass.
26 Details of hull construction:
A Mediterranean carvel construction.
B Atlantic clinker construction.
27 Wooden plane.
28 Wooden powder ram.
29 Muzzle-loading bronze gun.
30 Copper powder scoop.
31 Small muzzle loading gun.
A Cross section showing hail shot, wad and powder.

Spain and the Power of Gold

Spain and Portugal were the first European countries to embark on a systematic policy of discovery. Their aim was to find sea routes to the famed trade lands of eastern Asia. In the late fifteenth century the rivalry between them was intense. Though all educated people by then believed that the earth was round, Queen Isabella of Castile, patron of Columbus, was the only ruler with sufficient vision to finance an expedition to try to reach the Asian lands by sailing west. Columbus, who landed in the continent of America in 1492, set out to reach the Far East, and all his life believed that he had landed in China. The Spaniard Balboa crossed the Isthmus of Panama in 1513 and was the first European to see the Pacific Ocean. Only then was the staggering truth apparent: Spain possessed a vast new continent. It proved to contain enough gold and silver to make Spain, for a while, the greatest power in Europe.

The leader of Europe

Spain's new wealth confirmed its sense of national dignity. It had driven the Muslim forces from its soil in 1400. Spanish armies were feared everywhere. Spanish fashions and manners were copied. Spain was a cultural leader; a new university, which became one of Europe's finest, was founded at Alcalá' de Henares; Spanish writers and painters of this period, Lope de Vega, Cervantes, El Greco and later, Velazquez, are amongst the greatest of all time. Renaissance enthusiasm, coinciding with the influx of gold and silver from the New World, led to a burst of new building: new churches, hospitals, town halls and houses for the rich. Near his new capital, Madrid, Philip II built the magnificently sombre Escorial, a vast palace that was also a monastery and a royal tomb.

Living conditions in towns

The central feature of most Spanish towns was the Plaza Mayor, a large open square with colonnaded houses and public buildings. The roads opening from the square were often lined with small workshops and shops. In the south, in place of colonnades, awnings were hung from one building to the next to shade passers-by. Southern houses preserved the Arab plan, with a central patio on to which all the rooms opened. Further north, most houses had an entrance hall, a low room with an earth floor and light coming in from the doorway only. In richer houses this room was tiled and finely furnished. An upper floor contained living and reception rooms, and was little used except in cold weather; the hottest months were spent in the ground floor rooms, which were kept cool by sprinkling water on the flagstones.

Costume
1 A *hidalgo*, a member of the minor nobility.
2 Peasant women of Toledo. Her large felt hat shows an eastern influence.
3 Street dress of a young Spanish girl.

Cooking and eating utensils
4 It was customary to place a fig in a glass to sweeten water.
5 Earthenware water jar.
6 Silver candlestick.
7 Copper bucket.
8 Wooden bowl and spoon.
9 Wooden bellows.
10 Seville ware plates from the Armada wreck, *La Trinidad*, Valencera.
11 Portable stove, used indoors and out.
12 Tiled kitchen hearths, like this from El Greco's house, were traditionally wide enough to contain a shelf for sitting on either side.

El Greco's house

13 El Greco's library steps which convert to a chair. The artist would use them to reach up to the higher parts of his painting.

14 Cupboard.

15 Coffer and table from El Greco's house.

16 Sideboard in El Greco's house.

17 Paintbox from El Greco's house.

18 Copper brazier.

19 Cabinet on stand.

20 Velvet-covered trunk with sloping lid.

21 'X'-frame chair with leather back and seat.

22 Bedroom furniture in El Greco's house.

23 Wooden table with typical metal stretchers.

24 Low chair from El Greco's house.

25 Traditional peasant chair from El Greco's house.

26 Interior of El Greco's house, Toledo, in which the painter lived at intervals from 1585 till his death in 1614. Toledo, for centuries the artistic, industrial and commercial centre of Castile, retained a Moorish influence, which is seen in the plan and decorations of the house.

27 A and B, panel and frieze from the house, in the 'Mudejar' style, which combined Gothic and Islamic characteristics.

FIRST FLOOR

OFFICE
BEDROOM
ANTE ROOM
DRAWING ROOM
BALCONY
STUDIO
COURT
BALCONY
BALCONY

0   5   10 m

GROUND FLOOR

ENTRANCE
HALL
COURT
KITCHEN

21

The impoverished peasants

Most of the land belonged to the nobility or the church, neither of whom paid any taxes; these all fell on the common people. Success consisted in gaining a title and becoming a landowner. Unlike England, there was no middle class of merchants and professionals. Peasants rarely owned their own land. They were tenants of the great monasteries or of landowners in the towns. After paying tithes to the church and dues to their landlord, and reserving enough grain for seed, only half the peasants' crop remained.

Spain's decline

Unfortunately, Spain did not use its great wealth to ensure its own future prosperity. A huge proportion of it was spent on the wars that Charles V and Philip II fought to preserve Catholicism in Europe. The rest, which should have been invested in Spain's own industry and agriculture, was spent on buying luxuries abroad. The aristocratic leaders of the Spanish people, and those who tried to copy them, disdained manual work, which they associated with the despised *Moriscos* (followers of Islam who had become Christian in order to be allowed to remain in Spain). Spanish raw materials – wool and silk – were sent abroad to be manufactured. The industries of other European countries benefited while Spain's dwindled. After the expulsion of the industrious Moriscos, which began in 1609, the situation grew worse. By spending treasure abroad, and producing little of value itself, Spain enriched its rivals at the country's own expense. When the flow of American gold and silver shrank to a trickle, Spain was helpless.

Costume

1　Spanish nobleman. He wears a cloak with hanging sleeves and a sleeveless jerkin over his doublet. His trunks are padded.
2　A noblewoman. Her hair is rolled back over a pad and she wears a high masculine bonnet.
3　Boots fitted the leg tightly.
4　Women wore high 'chopines', a fashion that had come from the East, via Venice.
5　Shoes, usually with a narrow round toe, covered the whole foot. Heels were not known until 1600.
6　Outdoor over-shoes with cork soles.
7　Two-year-old prince. His baby skirts are as stiff as adult clothes.
8　A young princess. She wears adult court clothes.
9　Trunk hose in 'panes' or decorative panels, which show the lining beneath.

10　In Spain the ruff was worn very high under the ears.
11　The jerkin had a very high collar which turned the neck-band into a chin support.
12　The farthingale, which appeared in about 1545, was a conical underskirt stiffened by hoops of cane or whalebone. The farthingale emphasised social distinctions; it was not possible to do much work when wearing it.
13　The North European version of the farthingale held the skirts out over the hips by means of a padded roll.

Accessories

14　Attachment of sword and dagger to the belt.
15　A German pendant watch of about 1550: A open, B closed. Watches became the fashionable accessories of the rich. They were very inaccurate.

From the wreck of the *Girona*, a lost ship of the Armada
16　Pendant in the form of a golden salamander, set with rubies.
17　Gold cross of a Knight of Malta, belonging to the captain.
18　Lapis Lazuli cameo framed in enamelled gold, set with pearls.
19　Gold ring.
20　A jewelled cross made in the Spanish Indies, for export.
21　Silver forks.
Luxury goods
22　Glasses imported from Antwerp.
23　Earthenware dish from Talavera.
24　Silver jug.
25　Tin-glazed lustred earthenware 'refredador', a bottle for keeping liquids cool.
26　A double virginal made in Antwerp. Antwerp was famous for instrument making, exporting them to Spain and its colonies.

14

◁ Philip II
A   Philip II's invalid chair.
B   A gold escudo of Philip II's reign.
C   Philip II's dispatch case.

Spanish soldiers.
A   Infantryman.
B   Drummer.
C   Standard bearer.

American newcomers to Europe in the sixteenth century
A   Maize.
B   Tobacco.
C   Kidney beans.
D   Of a consignment of pineapples sent to Spain in the early sixteenth century, all were rotten but one, which was eaten by the king.
E   Sunflower from Florida.
F   The prickly pear astonished Europeans, who had never seen a cactus.
G   Agave. The Mexicans wove its fibres into fabric.
H   Tomato. Though it was used for cooking in Italy by the seventeenth century, it was regarded as poisonous in the north till much later.
I   Capsicums.
J   Cocoa. A slab form of chocolate was known in Spain by 1520. It was unpalatable when unsweetened and did not become a popular drink until sugar was plentiful.
K   The potato came to Spain in about 1570 but was not commonly cultivated until the eighteenth century.
L   Sweet potato.
M   Marrow and squash.
N   Turkeys. They were imported to Europe while the West Indies were still believed to lie off the shores of Asia, hence their name.

27   Sugar cane was introduced by the Arabs to Sicily and Spain but sugar remained a scarce luxury until cuttings were taken to the Caribbean and South America. The illustration shows sugar-syrup cooling and condensing into a block of crystals, in the traditional 'sugar-loaf' shape.
28   Inca foot-plough.

An Old-World Society in a New Environment

In April 1607, three little ships carried a hundred or so weary men up the mouth of the newly-named James River into a land that was unknown to them. Four months previously, they had sailed from London to form an English trading settlement in America. Spain would allow no other country to trade with its American colonies. Other countries had long been envious of Spain's overseas wealth, and, in the seventeenth century, the French, Dutch and English were all to compete with each other in claiming a share of the New World. Earlier English attempts in Virginia, pioneered by Sir Walter Raleigh, had failed through lack of organization and funds. Now a group of wealthy merchants and investors had formed the Virginia Company to finance this latest venture. They foresaw a good return for their money: the colony would supply luxuries and cheap raw materials and become a purchaser of English goods; gold and silver would be found, and a shorter route to Asia; the climate, similar to the Mediterranean, would produce lemons, oranges, sugar and spices; friendly Indians would exchange food for beads while the colonists mined gold.

Jamestown: the first settlement

With such hopes the settlers began to build their new home, choosing a riverside site with good anchorage for their ships, and a clear view downstream in case of Spanish attack. Mostly gentlemen, with no specific trades or skills, they had little ability to judge a site in terms of survival. The low-lying peninsula was swampy, covered with reedy grass and forest. The land had never been cleared; plainly the local people had not wanted it.

As they put up their first shelters in the humid, mosquito-infested summer the colonists succumbed to fevers and dysentery and very many died. Inexpertly, they felled trees and sawed clapboards to provide exports for homebound ships, which sailed in June leaving three months' supply of food. By August this contained 'as many worms as grain'. Winter came suddenly, with searing winds. The local Indians, friendly at first, were now unwilling to barter food. In summer they grew enough and to spare, but in winter they had no surplus. Their truculence was misinterpreted by the settlers; hostilities broke out and the settlers found that they were ill-equipped to deal with attacks by the Indians. The settlers' heavy armour, designed for open battle, was useless in the forest. With helmets closed they could see and hear little and were helpless targets for an ambush.

Arms and armour
1   Development of the musket.
A   Matchlock; a smouldering cord was brought into contact with powder by movement of the S-shaped arm.
B   Wheel-lock, devised in the sixteenth century: a wheel rotated against a piece of pyrites produced sparks which ignited the charge.
2   Scourer for cleaning the bore of a musket barrel.
3   Heavy armour. The settlers expected a Spanish attack.
4   Close helmet, found at Wolstenholme Towne.

▷   Jamestown, the first permanent English settlement in the New World. After Indian attacks the colonists replaced their first barriers of loose brushwood with a strong defensive fort. Rough timber-framed wattle and daub houses were reed-thatched. A kiln was set up to make chimney bricks. As life grew more secure the town spread beyond the fort, the site of which has since been washed away by the James River.
A   Church.
B   Guardhouse.
C   Storehouse.
At anchor are the vessels that brought the colonists: the *Discovery* (20 tonnes), *Godspeed* (40 tonnes), and *Susan Constant* (100 tonnes).

RIPE CORN

GREEN CORN

NEWLY PLANTED CORN

EATING PLACE

PRAYER FIRE

CEREMONIAL AREA

THE TOWN OF SECOTAN

THE TOWN OF POMEIOOC

Settlers and Indians

5 The governor of a hundred (a division of land).

6 Colonist in high armour. His 'brigantine' is lined with iron plates rivetted to the fabric. Powder containers hang from a bandolier. He carries a musket and a musket rest.

7 An Alconquian chieftain. The right side of his head is shaved to prevent entanglement with the bow-string. He wears a necklace of hammered copper beads (the Indians could not smelt metal). Copper was highly prized; in the 'starving time' the settlers exchanged a copper kettle for 80 bushels of maize.

8 Alconquian man and woman wearing skin cloaks. The child is carried in an Indian fashion.

9 Chieftain's wife and child. The mother carries a gourd jar and wears a necklace of shell beads, used as currency. The child has an English trade doll.

10 Chieftain's deerskin cloak decorated with marguiella shells.

11 Tobacco pipes:

A Indian, usually clay. A wood or cane stem might be attached.

B English clay pipe, made in imitation.

12 Indian clay cooking pot, steadied by heaps of earth.

13 Men and women ate facing each other from a wooden dish.

△ An Alconquian village. The Indians were skilful plant breeders and maize was sown. An Indian sits in the little shelter to scare away birds. Tobacco grows opposite. In the centre is the eating place. The prayer, fire and ceremonial areas are in the foreground.

▷ Some Indian villages were fortified. Alconquian houses were frameworks of bent saplings covered with bark or strips of matting. In summer the strips were rolled up to let in light and air. A shelf around the walls provided seating and sleeping space.

JAMESTOWN

STOREHOUSE

CHURCH

GUARDHOUSE

SUSAN CONSTANT

GODSPEED

DISCOVERY

New World farming

It was plain that, to survive, the settlers must grow their own food. With the haziest notions of agriculture (England, not needing to import agricultural products had not sent farming experts on the first ships) they cleared ground to grow wheat and barley. Their seed, selected for centuries to succeed in short northern summers, with long daylight hours, was unsuitable. After felling the dense forests, they found that tree roots needed years to rot; their ploughs were useless and traditional broadcast sowing a failure. Nothing came of their efforts.

Two Indian hostages eventually showed the settlers how to grow food. The Indians had cleared hundreds of acres without metal tools. They killed trees by ring-barking or root burning. Under the dead trees, small hillocks of earth were scraped up, and each was planted with four grains of maize and two beans. Pumpkins and sunflowers were also planted. In time, the area became a field, clear of forest growth. The settlers also learnt from the Indians how to trap animals and fish, barbecue meat and cook maize.

The 'starving time'

In the settlers' second winter, half the grain store was eaten by brown rats (which had arrived on the ships), or was found to be rotten. In 1609 came the terrible 'starving time'. After a great drought, neither settlers nor Indians had food. The settlers crawled out of the houses to catch snakes and eat 'strange roots'. Of 500, only 65 lasted the winter. The colonists sent an angry demand for skilled labourers back to England. Their struggle to survive had taught them the value of people who could make or do something useful.

Many of the next wave of settlers were indentured servants (bound by contract) hoping to become independent when they had worked the term agreed in their contract. Few realized their hopes, and many died of unnamed illnesses. From 1606 to 1625, 7,289 immigrants came to Virginia. During that time, 6,040 died.

A brighter future

In time, settlements spread along the James River and inland. Archaeologists have found traces of part of Wolstenholme Towne, headquarters of the region known as Martin's Hundred. The Towne was really a riverside village, where supplies were landed and goods stored prior to shipment. The settlers smelted iron, built ships and exported tar and timber. Then they discovered that Spanish-American tobacco would flourish, and was better than the local Indian variety. By 1619 over 2,000 kilos were exported; the future of the colony was assured.

1   Woman hackling (combing) flax.
2   Hair dressed over a wire roll, of a type found at the site.
3   One man's labour produced a tobacco crop worth six times the value of the wheat he could grow.
4   Scissors.
5   Wolstenholme Towne as it may have appeared from 1619 to 1622. The fort served the community as refuge from the Indians. The parapet-step enabled musketeers to fire over the palisade. The cannon, mounted to fire down-river, shows that Spanish attack was also expected. A street of houses, with a church, probably ran down to the water; their site has vanished through erosion of the river bank.

All from sites at Jamestown or Martin's Hundred
6   Brass thimble.
7A   Nickel alloy button.
B   Doublet from which it would have come.
8   Tenter hooks from a tenter frame for stretching cloth after fulling.

DOMESTIC UNIT

KITCHEN GARDEN

MAIZE FIELD

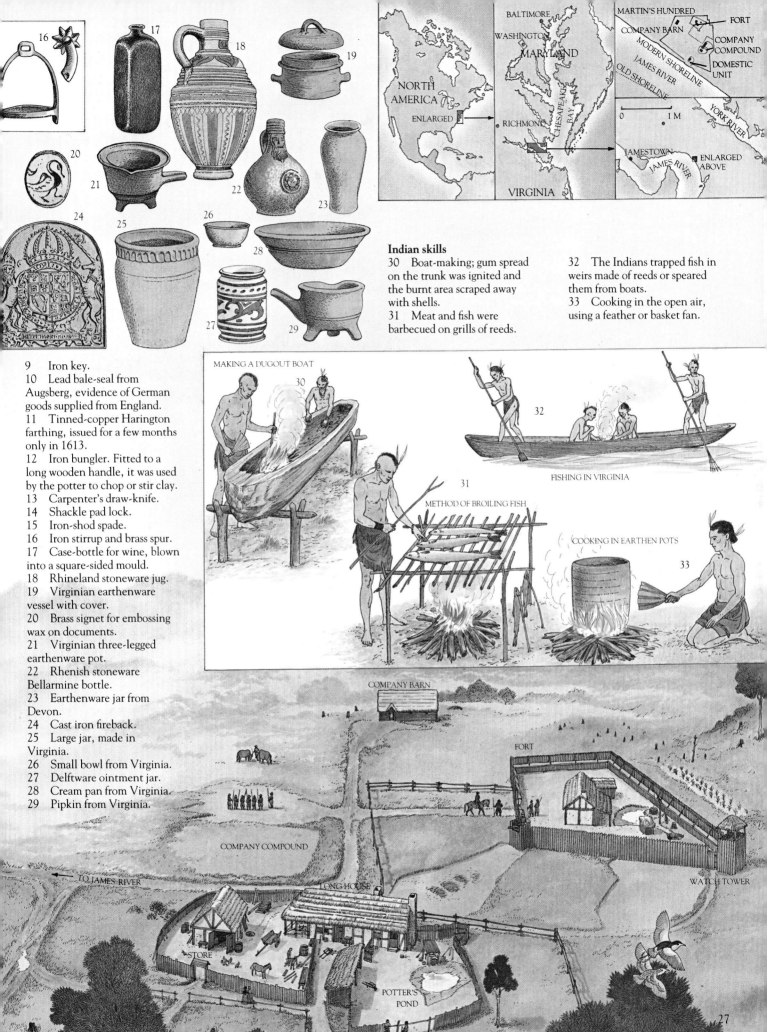

Indian skills

30 Boat-making; gum spread on the trunk was ignited and the burnt area scraped away with shells.

31 Meat and fish were barbecued on grills of reeds.

32 The Indians trapped fish in weirs made of reeds or speared them from boats.

33 Cooking in the open air, using a feather or basket fan.

9 Iron key.

10 Lead bale-seal from Augsberg, evidence of German goods supplied from England.

11 Tinned-copper Harington farthing, issued for a few months only in 1613.

12 Iron bungler. Fitted to a long wooden handle, it was used by the potter to chop or stir clay.

13 Carpenter's draw-knife.

14 Shackle pad lock.

15 Iron-shod spade.

16 Iron stirrup and brass spur.

17 Case-bottle for wine, blown into a square-sided mould.

18 Rhineland stoneware jug.

19 Virginian earthenware vessel with cover.

20 Brass signet for embossing wax on documents.

21 Virginian three-legged earthenware pot.

22 Rhenish stoneware Bellarmine bottle.

23 Earthenware jar from Devon.

24 Cast iron fireback.

25 Large jar, made in Virginia.

26 Small bowl from Virginia.

27 Delftware ointment jar.

28 Cream pan from Virginia.

29 Pipkin from Virginia.

MAKING A DUGOUT BOAT

FISHING IN VIRGINIA

METHOD OF BROILING FISH

COOKING IN EARTHEN POTS

NORTH AMERICA

ENLARGED

BALTIMORE

WASHINGTON

MARYLAND

RICHMOND

CHESAPEAKE BAY

VIRGINIA

MARTIN'S HUNDRED

COMPANY BARN

MODERN SHORELINE

JAMES RIVER

OLD SHORELINE

FORT

COMPANY COMPOUND

DOMESTIC UNIT

YORK RIVER

0   1 M

JAMESTOWN

JAMES RIVER

ENLARGED ABOVE

COMPANY BARN

FORT

COMPANY COMPOUND

TO JAMES RIVER

LONG HOUSE

STORE

POTTER'S POND

WATCH TOWER

27

France: Design for Living

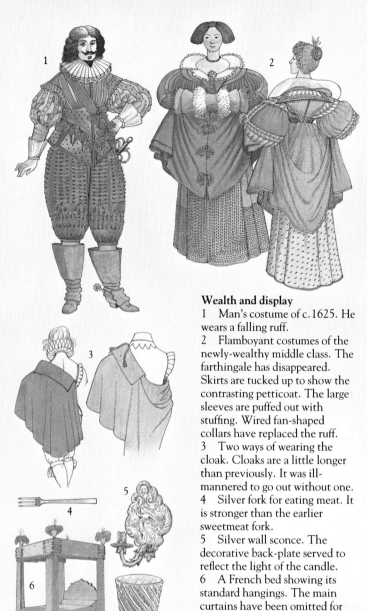

In early seventeenth-century France the arts of elegant town life were developed and refined. For the next three centuries French fashions in dress, furnishings and manners were copied by the rest of the western world. Paris developed as the centre of civilized life and thought. It possessed at this period the most brilliant group of Frenchmen in all fields that have ever appeared at one time. In philosophy it was the age of Descartes, in religion Pascal, in drama Corneille, Molière and Racine, in painting Poussin and Claude, and in architecture François Mansart.

The rebuilding of Paris

The face of Paris was rapidly transformed. Already one of the largest towns in Europe, it became the most carefully designed and harmoniously planned. Its old wooden bridges were rebuilt in stone. The Pont Neuf was the first thoroughfare to have wide pavements for pedestrians. A succession of fashionable new residential areas was built, beginning with ambitious projects of Henry IV: the Place Dauphine, the Place Royale (now the Place des Vosges) and the unfinished Place de France. In these the Renaissance ideals of architectural regularity and proportion were applied for the first time to the layout of domestic buildings. The King leased individual plots of land on condition that the tenant built according to an agreed plan – the first townscaping of private houses in Europe.

Order and convenience

Inside the houses, much thought was given to order and convenience. As yet, only the richest people employed architects but many were interested in the new ideas of rational planning. Pattern books were produced, giving advice on ground plans and the distribution of rooms, from which the client could direct his builder. The ideal apartment would have a reception room opening into an ante-chamber, which in turn opened into the bedchamber. This room was not the equivalent of a modern bedroom. Its function was a survival of the medieval usage in which the room in which a person's bed stood was his private reception room, where honoured visitors and intimate friends were received. One or more small private rooms, called closets, opened from the bedchamber.

The little closets provided studies, dressing rooms, or primitive lavatories. Bathrooms were rare before the 1670s, so bathtubs were brought into the apartments. The ceremonial state apartment did not normally have an occupant. It contained the *lit de parade* or state bed. This was a symbol reflecting the high status of the owner or his visitors.

Wealth and display
1   Man's costume of c.1625. He wears a falling ruff.
2   Flamboyant costumes of the newly-wealthy middle class. The farthingale has disappeared. Skirts are tucked up to show the contrasting petticoat. The large sleeves are puffed out with stuffing. Wired fan-shaped collars have replaced the ruff.
3   Two ways of wearing the cloak. Cloaks are a little longer than previously. It was ill-mannered to go out without one.
4   Silver fork for eating meat. It is stronger than the earlier sweetmeat fork.
5   Silver wall sconce. The decorative back-plate served to reflect the light of the candle.
6   A French bed showing its standard hangings. The main curtains have been omitted for clarity.
7   Gold drinking goblet.

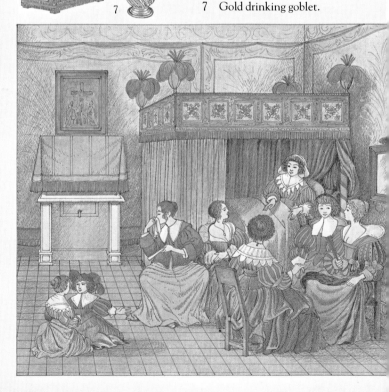

◁ The Pont de la Tournelle before its reconstruction.

▷ The Ile Saint Louis with the Pont Marie on the left and the Pont de la Tournelle on the right. The island was created by joining two islets, the Ile au Vaches and the Ile Notre-Dame. Large dignified houses for the very wealthy were built there during the second quarter of the century.

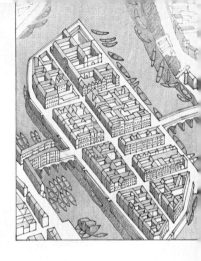

Transport
13 Coaches, in use since the sixteenth century, were now more common. The best were made in France. They were distinguished from the covered wagon by having the body suspended by straps, to reduce jolting.

Furniture
14 A 'buffet' with cupboard above and drawers below. Its doors are inset with geometric mouldings.
15 A wooden baby-walker.

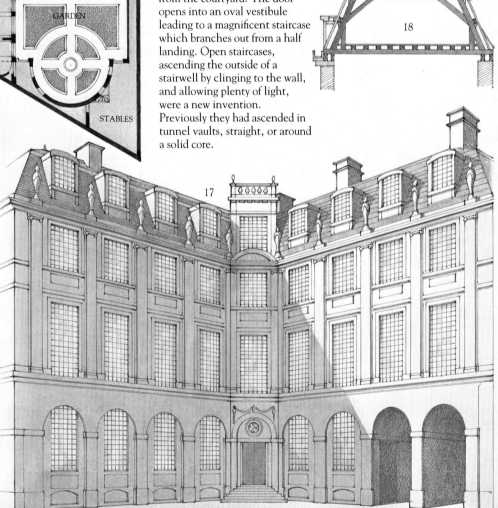

16

GRAND STAIRCASE

KITCHEN

COACH HOUSE

SALON (DRAWING ROOM)

COURTYARD

GARDEN

STABLES

Monsieur Roland's House
16 Ground plan of a house and garden designed for M. Roland, in the rue Clery, Montmartre, in the 1620s. The street wing contains servants' workspace. The courtyard wing has a reception room leading to smaller rooms overlooking the garden. A grand staircase leads to the main apartments on the first floor.
17 View of M. Roland's house from the courtyard. The door opens into an oval vestibule leading to a magnificent staircase which branches out from a half landing. Open staircases, ascending the outside of a stairwell by clinging to the wall, and allowing plenty of light, were a new invention. Previously they had ascended in tunnel vaults, straight, or around a solid core.

18 Section of a mansard roof, named after François Mansart, though not invented by him. The upper section of a pitched roof is not useful space; in the mansard the top is cut off giving a lower mass, more easily harmonized with the building below.

18

17

8 Gold cross, set with emeralds and decorated with enamel and pearl pendants.
9 Gilt metal table clock and leather carrying case. The clock strikes the hours and has an alarm. It belonged to the Duc d'Orleans, brother of Louis XIII.
10 Candlestick of tooled silver.
11 Silver cup in two halves, with a filter for infusing a drink.
12 A carved ebony cabinet on stand. The doors conceal a number of drawers.

◁ A visit to a new mother, from an engraving by Abraham Bosse. It shows a Parisian woman receiving visitors in her bedchamber in the 1630s. The covered cabinet is probably a house altar. The mirror is nailed to the wall through the tapestry hangings. The floor is laid with squares of parquet.

1 Fashionable Paris
1 The parlour of an elegant Paris town house in the 1640s. The most important feature is the fireplace. Its large ball-topped fire dogs are ornamental; the logs are supported by smaller dogs, further in. The stiff low-backed chairs are typical of the time; they still show Spanish influence. They are ranged in a row along the wall; the centres of rooms were empty of furniture unless it was in use. Only the bottom sections of the sash windows open, as there are not yet any counterbalancing weights. The curtains are for protection against sunlight, not for warmth. Deep lace-trimmed falling collars and cuffs are now worn by men and women. Men have shoulder-length hair and wear their hats indoors.

Country life
2 Peasant costume of the Champagne area, second half of the seventeenth century. The man wears a neck cloth and a plain coat which has replaced the doublet. The woman wears the traditional 'bagnolet' head-dress.
3 Large iron cooking pot.
4 Pewter jug for holding hot water for shaving.
5 Pedlar.
6 Waterseller.
7 Traditional baskets. The tall one, carried on the back, transported grapes and other goods. The large 'panier mannequin' collected champagne grapes for transport to the press.
8 A vinegar seller.
9 Pastry cook's metal tart moulds.
10 Basketwork face screen for shielding the face when sitting near the large open fires.
11 Bottle of thin glass, protected by wicker, which transferred wine or vinegar from the cask to the table.

An apartment was the living quarters of one person; well-to-do husbands and wives usually had separate apartments symmetrically arranged on either side of an entrance vestibule. Poorer people lived in one room with a bed in it and a closet opening off. A great house was divided into three areas; one for ceremonial purposes, one in which the family lived and one in which the servants worked. The first and second were sometimes on different sides of the house, but more usually on different floors. Children and senior staff had inferior rooms tucked out of the way. Servants lived in the attics, or over the stables.

Interior decoration
Though chairs were still stiff and thinly upholstered, there was much attention to comfort in the luxurious hangings of walls and bed curtains. A new piece of furniture, the day bed (a long seat with a headrest at one end, usually placed in a corner) testifies to the idea of relaxing in company. The idea of a unified scheme of decoration was introduced from Italy by the literary hostess Madame de Rambouillet. She caused a sensation in Paris in the 1620s when the room in which she received her visitors was painted blue with blue velvet hangings patterned in gold, with all the chairs and the carpet over the table to match.

Conditions in the countryside
The elegant town life of the wealthy bourgeois was a world apart from the conditions of the peasants in the countryside, for whom one bad harvest could bring starvation. In France nearly all the land was divided into *seigneuries* (roughly equivalent to the English manor). A seigneurie comprised of two kinds of property: the *domaine proche* which the *seigneur* (lord) cultivated for his own use with paid labour, and the *mouvance* which was inhabited by peasants who were said to own it. They could not be evicted and could sell or bequeath their share, but in reality they owned only the right to use the land. The true owner was the seigneur and in recognition of this they owed him feudal dues and services.

These peasant proprietors were very numerous and often owned plots too small to support a family adequately. In addition to feudal dues they had to pay the *taille*, a tax levied on all commoners. In practice, it fell largely on the peasants because exemptions had been granted to people living in the towns.

While bad harvests brought starvation to the peasants, the rise in agricultural prices brought profits to the large landowners and merchants. They also benefited from the increasing acreage devoted to vineyards. In 1627 Louis XIII forbade new plantations. Too much vine-growing was causing a shortage of corn.

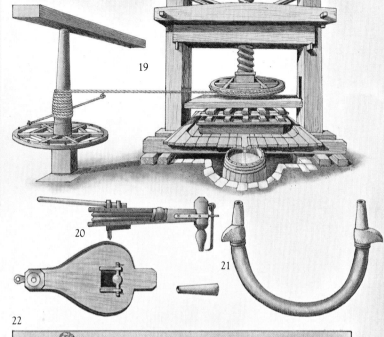

△ A view of the town of Ay, in the seventeenth century. There are vineyards all around. The wines of Ay were among the most famous of the Champagne area.

Wine-making

14 A 'danderlin', a staved wooden receptacle for transporting wine to the cellars.

15-17 Wooden and metal wine tasting cups.

18 Pruning knife.

19 A champagne press. The champagne method requires grapes to be pressed in a thin layer. The grapes were placed in the shallow receptacle made of wooden staves which could be taken out for cleaning. Peasants were required to press their wine and grapes in their seigneur's mill. They were not allowed to sell their own wine until the seigneurs and the monks had sold theirs.

20-21 Bellows (front and side view) and hose used to pump the must (grape juice) from the press.

22 A late seventeenth-century inn. The woman is bringing the traditional wicker-covered bottle to be filled.

Champagne

12 Seventeenth-century champagne bottles and (13) glass. Until the mid-century only thin, fragile bottles were available, suitable for bringing wine from the cask to the table, not for transporting it. These were stoppered with wood wrapped in oiled hemp. In the 1660s a new technique of glass blowing produced strong bottles capable of withstanding the pressure of fermentation. The champagne method was perfected by using these bottles and stoppering them with corks.

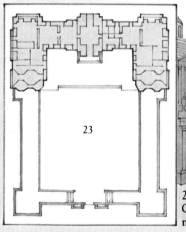

23 Ground plan of the Chateau Maisons. Only the main building survives.

24 The chateau of Maisons near Paris. It was designed by François Mansart c.1642–6.

The Dutch: a New Nation

The Dutch were a very new nation in the seventeenth century. The Netherlands had been part of the Spanish Empire until the seven northern provinces broke away to become a self-governing Protestant country in 1648. Because the land had few natural resources, its people had for centuries relied on trade for survival. They were industrious and resourceful, excellent fishermen, shipbuilders and merchants. By the mid-century they were the richest people in Europe. Dutch merchants of the East India Company imported luxuries from Asia, and Amsterdam became the market place of the world.

Amsterdam: a storehouse for Europe

Amsterdam's wealth depended upon the grain trade. The population of Europe had grown so much during the sixteenth century that many countries could no longer grow enough grain to feed all their people. They had to import more from the vast grain-growing regions of Poland. Dutch ships collected the grain from the Baltic ports and brought it to Amsterdam. From there it was re-exported all over Europe. Amsterdam became a great storehouse, not only of grain but of all sorts of other goods, because it was a convenient place to exchange merchandise.

Dutch peoples' prosperity was also due to their skill in using technology to solve practical problems. They used wind-powered drainage mills to drain marshy land and to reclaim large areas from the sea. The network of canals needed to carry the water away provided a much quicker and cheaper means of transport than the rough unmade roads of those days. Passenger barges sailed between towns according to a fixed timetable.

Housing in towns

Because the cost of reclaimed land was high, Dutch town houses were tall in proportion to their ground area. The narrow gable end usually faced the street. The stairs were so steep and winding that goods and furniture had to be hoisted in through the windows by means of a great hook and pulley in the gable. In the older houses the door opened directly into the front room, which often served as a shop or workshop. A merchant might have his office on the ground floor of his house and his goods stored in the cellar or in the double loft. Most houses were simply furnished in the earlier part of the century. Their most splendid pieces of furniture were large storage cupboards for linen and household articles. But as the country grew richer, people liked to display their wealth through the number of their possessions. They bought elaborately inlaid furniture, paintings and oriental porcelain.

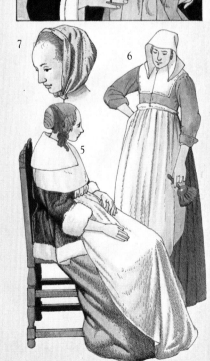

Costume

1 A fashionable Dutchman of about 1660. His very short doublet shows his shirt at the waist. His breeches, known as 'rhiengraves', are so wide that they look like a skirt; they are decorated with falling ribbons at the top.

2 A fashionable woman. Her bodice, pointed at the waist, left the shoulders almost bare; the neckline might be filled with a lace collar or scarf or by the edge of the chemise.

3 Bodices were often fastened down the back.

4 The sober dress of a 'regent' family. The woman wears a descendant of the medieval cap which the Dutch were the last to abandon. It is held in place by a rigid wire. The regents were a small group of long established merchant families who held the most important political positions and kept power in their hands. Though very rich they believed in the traditional Dutch virtues of simplicity and restraint.

5 This housewife wears the short velvet jacket, trimmed with swan's down. She has tied her apron over it. She also wears a deep double starched collar.

6 Woman wearing a loose bonnet with hanging ends.

7 It could also be worn tied under the chin.

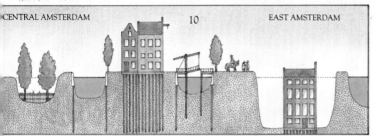

CENTRAL AMSTERDAM 10 EAST AMSTERDAM

△ The main highways of Amsterdam were canals with roads, often tree lined, on either side. One of the most decorative features of the houses was the gable ends. As fashions in gables changed, houses were brought up to date by altering the gables.

A The medieval houses were of timber but after 1500 brick became common and stepped gables were built.
B,C,D Seventeenth-century gable types. The large shuttered opening in the top floor of D is a doorway through which goods were hauled.

8   Detail of house foundations. The peaty ground on which Amsterdam stands had posed no problems for the light timber houses of the middle ages, but in order to support masonry buildings it was necessary to drive piles down about 10 metres to reach the firm sandy subsoil. The double stakes were held together by nailed boards and wooden cross-ties. The foundations could cost as much as the house.

9   Interior construction of the gable.

10   Cross section of Amsterdam showing house foundations, canals, embankments and later developments below sea level.

11   Section through the house of a prosperous merchant in the second half of the seventeenth century. It was common to have a mezzanine floor lit by the upper half of the tall ground floor windows. This helped to conserve warmth in the room below. The rooms are quite elaborately furnished. Pictures and porcelain ornaments display the owner's wealth. In the reception room the end of a French bed is just visible, showing that the owners followed fashion. This would be for visitors' use. The family slept upstairs in traditional Dutch cupboard beds. Above are a laundry room and a store room where peat and logs are also kept. The peat fire in the hearth is built up in a cylinder shape to give ventilation for burning. The chimney breast is cut away below the mantle shelf; a cloth pelmet helps direct the smoke upwards. Behind the house is a small yard and a scullery building.

12   Ground plan of the house.

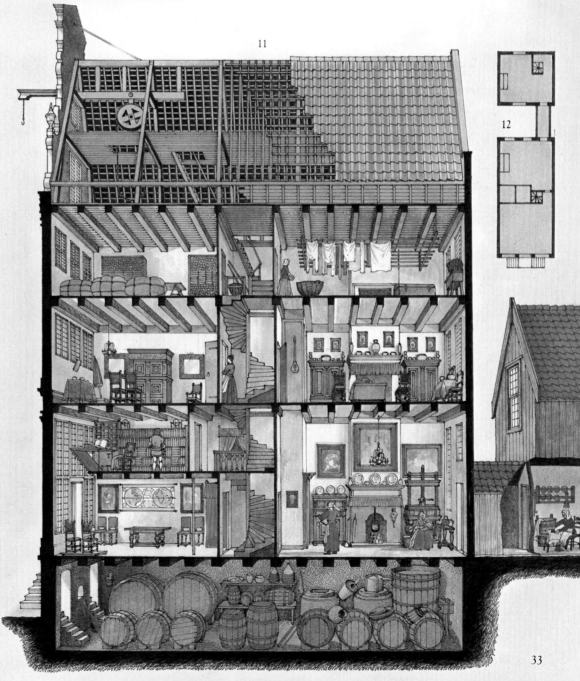

Furniture and porcelain
1   Oak dining table with extending leaves.
2   Linen press.
3   Velvet-covered chair with padded seat and back.
4   Child's chair with chamber pot in base.
5   A backgammon board.
6   A paint box and easel. An enormous number of pictures were sold to decorate house walls.
7   Foot warmer with a brazier of charcoal.
8   A The earliest pendulum clocks were made in the Hague.
9   Sunshades were brought home from the East by traders of the Dutch East India Company.
10 Soft house broom.
11 Delft jug of tin-glazed earthenware.
12 Glassware: A Flute glass. B 'Roamer', a German wine cup. C   Diamond engraved goblet.
13 Pewter flagon.
14 Chinese stoneware teapot with gilt mounts added in Europe. Tea was brought back from China by the East India Company early in the century.
15 Chinese porcelain, brought back by the East India Company, was greatly admired. The secret of making it was unknown in the West. It was imitated by tin-glazed earthenware, made at Delft.
A   Delft tiles.
B   Delftware with cover.
16 Silver-gilt salt cellar.
17 Smoker's equipment.

The front room became a reception room which was scarcely used for fear of disturbing its perfect order. Family life took place in the living room or kitchen. Dutch housewives were very houseproud. The mistress of the house usually did the housework and shopping herself, with the aid of a maidservant. There were fewer servants in the Netherlands than elsewhere.

A carefully-planned new town

Visitors noted how clean and well run Dutch towns were. Amsterdam had one-way streets and restrictions on private coaches in the centre of the town. There was public street lighting by oil lamps. Of course, there were also slums. Many people lived in tiny cramped houses in the back alleys or rented a cellar or an attic. Because the city was so overcrowded it was greatly enlarged in the early part of the century. The extension was carefully planned; three new canals ringed the old town, widely spaced so that the houses could have deep gardens behind. The new building plots were bought by wealthy merchants. Industries were banned from these residential areas.

In comparison with other nations at this time, a much larger proportion of Dutch people were town dwellers. The reclaimed lands were very fertile so it became exceedingly profitable to specialize in growing fruit and vegetables to meet the demands of the towns. These farms often belonged to city merchants, because they had the money to invest in drainage schemes. Peasant smallholders became tenants or sought work in the towns.

Peasant farming

Peasant farming continued on the poorer soils in the eastern part of the country. The traditional farmhouse combined barn and dwelling space under one roof. At one end of the building was the threshing floor, with a hay loft above and a doorway wide enough to admit a farm wagon; at the other was the open hearth. The woman of the house could sit at her spinning while keeping an eye on the cooking pot, the livestock and the family at work in the barn, and could give orders without stirring from her seat. Smoke rising from the fire dried and preserved the harvest in the loft. Cows and sheep were kept for their manure, which was essential to improve the sandy soil. Most of the produce – wool for clothing and rye for bread – was needed for the household, though there might be a little over to sell to provide money with which to buy luxuries. Some produce was given as payment to landless labourers and craftsmen. They worked in return for food and the use of horses, ploughs and wagons. As a result, the villages formed close-knit communities, living frugally, but avoiding dire poverty.

Tools and equipment

18   Baker's display which hung outside his shop.
19   A chaff-cutting machine for cutting up straw for fodder.
20   Kettle.
21   A chopper and wooden bowl for chopping vegetables.
22   Round-bottomed earthenware cooking pot.
23   Peasant's rough wooden table.

24   (right) The Republic of the Netherlands and its neighbours. The green area shows the land that needed drainage.
25   A drainage mill. The rotating screw scooped up the water and raised it to a higher level.

26   Traditional three-legged chair.
27   Child's chair.
28   Rush-seated chair.
29   Fire guard.
30   Ox collar.
31   Pot crane.
32   Commode.
33   Birch broom.
34   Turf cutter.
35   Threshing stick.
36   Flail.
37   Pitchfork.
38   Peasant farmstead. Behind is a hay barrack.

Peasant living conditions

39   Interior of a farmhouse. By the seventeenth century, rooms began to be made at the dwelling end. The floor was of mud.
40   Gable end.
41   Poor peasants still ate from wooden plates, though many people could now afford pewter and the rich dined from porcelain.
42   A peasant family at supper.
43   Unglazed earthenware oil lamp.

44   Day labourer's cabin. There were many casual workers, peat cutters and farm hands, too poor to afford a house. They lived in dugout huts with roof and walls cut from the peat.
45   Sheep cote used to house sheep at night to collect the all-important dung.
46   A bakehouse. These were built separately because of fires.
46A   Cross section of the bakehouse.

NORTH SEA
NORWICH
GRONINGEN
ENGLAND
ZUIDER ZEE
MUNSTER
AMSTERDAM
THE HAGUE
UTRECHT
ROTTERDAM
ARNHEM
DORTMUND
BRUGES
ANTWERP
DUSSELDORF
GHENT
LILLE
BRUSSELS
COLOGNE
SPANISH NETHERLANDS
AIX-LA-CHAPELLE
CHARLEROI
RIVER RHINE
FRANCE

New England: Farmers and Traders

By the end of the seventeenth century, settlements were scattered along a thousand miles of the eastern coast of North America, from Maine to South Carolina. By 1690, the population of the English colonies numbered just over 200,000. The characteristics of each colony varied according to its founder's intentions, and these plans were in turn altered by the nature of the land itself.

Early Puritan settlements

The Puritans who founded the first New England colonies wanted to establish small farming communities in which they could live and worship in a simple, 'purified' way. They had no intention of founding cities. Whenever a township grew too large some members set off to form a new community elsewhere. Their townships had many things in common with an English village. Houses were not scattered on the land being farmed but grouped together around the 'open lot' or common, near a convenient stream or spring. Each stood in its 'home lot', a small plot containing outbuildings – woodshed, privy and barn – vegetable patch, herb garden and orchard. The village had no manor house and no church of the kind known in England. These symbols of authority were replaced by the meeting house, a plain square building in which people met to worship and to discuss community affairs.

Next to the meeting house stood the Sabbath house, one end containing a stable, the other a large room with a fireplace. Here those who had come long distances could shelter their horses, cook their dinner and warm up at midday. Nearby was the minister's house and perhaps a one-room schoolhouse. The garrison house, unknown in an English village, was a vitally important building, since increasing settlement caused conflict with the dispossessed Indians. All men possessed weapons and had to serve in the militia.

The settlers built the sort of houses they were familiar with in the villages of south-eastern England; timber box frames with brick or wattle and daub infilling. Thus the New World preserved a tradition that was dying out in England, where supplies of timber were being exhausted for ship building and to supply charcoal for iron smelting. The oak frame of each settler house was sheathed in clapboarding – horizontal overlapping boards which provided insulation essential in the hard climate. The roofs were covered with shingles of pine. A cellar dug beneath the house kept provisions cool in summer and protected them from frost in winter.

Puritan costume and furniture
1 A Puritan gentleman of the late seventeenth century.
2 His wife wears a simple gown with a long full apron.
3 Outdoor costume of a tradeswoman and child.
4 A man on his way to work.
5 Child's turned highchair of maplewood.
6 Oak and pine cradle.
7 Oak and pine box, originally painted red.
8 Pottery imported from England:
A Slipware plate from North Devon
B Lambeth bowl of tin-glazed earthenware.
9 A court cupboard, dated 1680, used for storing linen and displaying fine dishes and silver.
10 Oak spice chest, dated 1679.
11 Silver tankard made in Massachusetts.
12 Slipware cup from North Devon.
13 White pine settle.
14 Wooden bed wrench for tightening bedropes when they sagged.

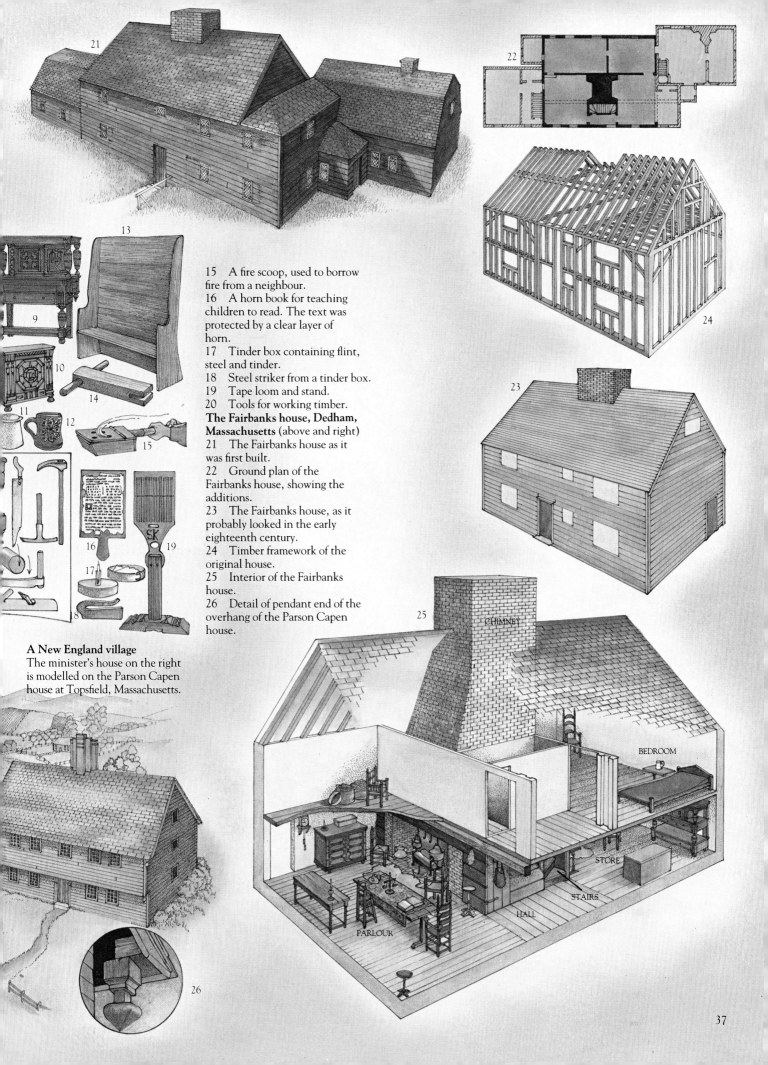

15   A fire scoop, used to borrow fire from a neighbour.

16   A horn book for teaching children to read. The text was protected by a clear layer of horn.

17   Tinder box containing flint, steel and tinder.

18   Steel striker from a tinder box.

19   Tape loom and stand.

20   Tools for working timber.

The Fairbanks house, Dedham, Massachusetts (above and right)

21   The Fairbanks house as it was first built.

22   Ground plan of the Fairbanks house, showing the additions.

23   The Fairbanks house, as it probably looked in the early eighteenth century.

24   Timber framework of the original house.

25   Interior of the Fairbanks house.

26   Detail of pendant end of the overhang of the Parson Capen house.

A New England village

The minister's house on the right is modelled on the Parson Capen house at Topsfield, Massachusetts.

CHIMNEY

BEDROOM

STORE

STAIRS

HALL

PARLOUR

37

1A and B Massachusetts paper money printed on parchment. Paper money was first printed by the colony in 1690.

American Silver

2 Tea caddy, c.1725, made in New York.
3 Silver sugar box, c. 1710.
4 Sugar cutters.
5 Silver teapot, made 1710-20, in Newfoundland.
6 Silver chocolate pot, made in Boston.
7 Silver spout cup, for feeding invalids, made in New York early 1700 s.
8 Silver drinking bowl 1680-1700, made in New York.

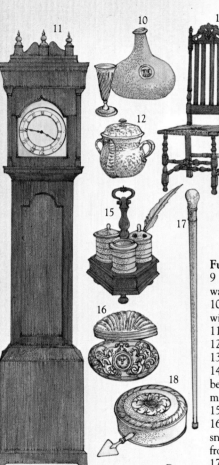

Furniture and fashions

9 Serving table, veneered in walnut with slate top. c. 1700.
10 Wine glass, c. 1700, and wine bottle of 1720.
11 American long-case clock.
12 English Delftware posset pot.
13 Maple chair, c. 1720.
14 A folding bed, showing the bed cords which supported the mattress.
15 Walnut and brass inkstand.
16 Silver and cockle-shell snuff-box, perhaps imported from England or Holland.
17 Ivory handled cane.
18 Silver patch box and trowel.
19 Wigs were worn in America, just as much as in Europe.
A Bag wig.
B Knotted wig.
C White pipeclay wig curlers.
D Wig stand.
20 Brass comb.
21 Two Spanish razors in a case.

The earliest houses usually had two rooms upstairs and down, with a central brick or stone chimney which provided a fireplace for each. The hall was a combined living, cooking and dining room. Its hearth was the centre of life throughout the long winter. The logs used to keep the family warm were sometimes so big that they were dragged in through the back door by a horse. Even so, people recorded the ink freezing on their pens as they wrote by the fire. The parlour next door was used for special occasions. Both rooms might serve as bedrooms, in addition to those upstairs. Space was short; beds were hinged to fold against the wall and ladder-backed chairs were hung on pegs when not in use. More room could be gained by adding a lean-to at the back. The lean-to's central section was usually a kitchen, with a bake-oven opening from the main chimney. The rooms on either side were used as a pantry and as an extra bedroom.

Trapping, fishing and trading

By the end of the century the Puritan ideal of simple living had developed in a way that the first settlers had not foreseen. Of necessity, they had become farmers but the soil was infertile and they very soon realized that the real wealth of the land lay in its forests and seas. The Puritans soon added to their income by fishing and trading with the Indians for furs. As traders, they grew wealthy from dealings in salt cod, furs, rum, timber and ships' masts exported to the English colonies, to England and the West Indies. Ports grew up along the indented coastline with ship yards to provide vessels for the ever-increasing trade. By the 1720s Boston had become a busy seaport of 10,000 people, the largest in the colonies. Yet in some respects it remained, until well into the eighteenth century, a medieval town. Its wealthy citizens, more interested in trade than town planning, were satisfied with dwellings that were larger versions of the original clap-board house. Boston's narrow streets followed the pattern of the paths between the farm lots of the original village.

An elegant and prosperous way of life

Wealthy New Englanders appreciated comfort and refinement within their homes, and could well afford them. Specialist colonial craftsmen were now producing all manner of furniture and luxury goods. The finest furniture, china, glass and carpets were imported from England. Fashion was said to cross the Atlantic quicker than it reached the further parts of Britain. In 1700 a Boston bookseller advertised sheets of painted paper for walls – a French idea, newly arrived. The elegance and prosperity of New England city life would have amazed its Puritan forefathers.

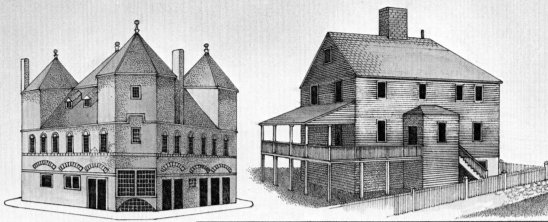

△ The triangular warehouse, Boston, built in brick after the great fire of 1679. It stood at the top of North Market Street. It was demolished in 1824.

◁ The Jonathan Sayward House, York, Maine. Very few buildings and no large merchant's houses of seventeenth-century Boston survive, due to several bad fires. This house, built in c. 1720, is still in existence, almost unaltered, and gives a good idea of the kind of house a prosperous Boston merchant would have lived in. It is unpretentious but quite large and comfortable.

▷ Interior of the sitting room of the Jonathan Sayward House as it might have been when newly built. The walls are panelled and the sash windows have wooden glazing bars. The occupants are enjoying the new ceremony of taking tea in the afternoon. They sit at a table which has been brought out for the occasion. It has a tilt top and would normally be folded up at the side of the room. The tea kettle is on a stand beside the table; the cups have no handles.

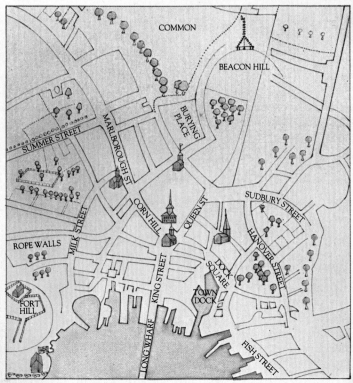

△ Boston's Old Town House destroyed by fire in 1711. A market was held under it.

◁ Map of Boston in 1728 showing its many wharves. Long Wharf, built 1710-13, provided for 30 large vessels. It was lined with shops and warehouses.

△ The New Town House, built in 1713. It housed the town and provincial government courts and the merchant's exchange. The interior was burnt out in 1747.

France: A Pre-Revolutionary Aristocrat

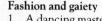

The life enjoyed by the wealthiest French aristocrats before the Revolution was one of the most civilized and luxurious that Europe has known. It was a life which few, even among the nobility, could afford. The nobles were a privileged class, exempt from most of the taxes levied on townspeople and peasants on the grounds that they were supposed to defend the king with their swords. They saw themselves as representing the old feudal chivalry, though many were the descendants, only a few generations removed, of ennobled financiers, or of lawyers who had bought entry into the nobility.

Nobles at court

The nobleman's status forbade him to take part in trade or industry. His income depended almost entirely on rents and dues from his estates or on obtaining a position or pension from the king. Louis XIV created a magnificent court at Versailles. It became essential for a nobleman to be seen at the court and to cut a fine figure there. It was the King's policy to encourage expensive fashions so that the nobles were in perpetual need of money and had to beg favours from him. Noblemen struggled to put by enough money to spend two or three weeks a year at Versailles. Some ruined themselves in their efforts to compete.

Domestic elegance

Louis XV, who succeeded his grandfather, Louis XIV, was a shy man. He devised another, more private, style of living which quickly became fashionable in smart society. He still went through the motions of the *levée* and *couchée* (the public ceremonials of going to bed and rising in the great royal bedchamber) just as Louis XIV had done, but when the last courtier had left he got out of bed, put on his dressing gown and returned to his comfortable small apartments. In the evenings, he liked to withdraw to a small private room with only a few friends, and to have his supper brought in and served there. It was the greatest honour to be admitted to these little supper parties. Supper was followed by card games while the King made his own coffee.

Fashionable Parisians quickly copied this more intimate style of living. Houses were planned for comfort and informal entertaining. They were still luxuriously furnished, with many suites of rooms for use at different times of the day. Panelled walls were elaborately carved and gilded with twirling Rococo decoration. Rooms sometimes had curved corners and coved ceilings.

Fashion and gaiety
1 A dancing master holding a pochette – a miniature violin which can be slipped into a pocket while he demonstrates a step.
2 Fashionable clothes of the 1750s. The woman's skirt is held out by a hooped petticoat. The man's coat, with deep divided cuffs, has become narrower.
Luxury goods
3 Enamelled gold chatelaine with pendant watch and loops for additional objects.
4 Glass scent flask, or smelling bottle, with gold and enamel stopper, and its case.
5 Porcelain-handled brush from a toilet service.
6 Umbrella maker's advertisement showing an umbrella with a collapsible handle and a cover. Umbrellas of oiled silk had been in use since the beginning of the century.
7 A Parisian bathroom. The copper bath has an elegant wooden stand. The canopy could be drawn to make a steam tent. The lady is wearing her chemise in the bath. The custom of lining the bath with a cloth survives from the need for protection against splinters in a wooden tub.

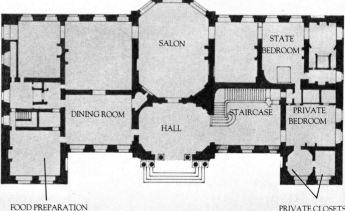

SALON

STATE BEDROOM

DINING ROOM

HALL

STAIRCASE

PRIVATE BEDROOM

FOOD PREPARATION

PRIVATE CLOSETS

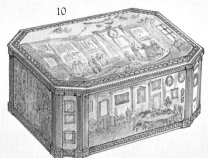

High-society elegance

8 The Duc de Choiseul, foreign minister of Louis XV, from a portrait by Louis-Michel van Loo. He wears a tie-wig with 'pigeons wings' (bunches of curls over the ears).

9 A woman at her dressing table. She wears a dressing cape and is putting a patch on her face from the patch box in her hand. Patches were used to cover spots or to draw attention to a fine complexion.

A world in miniature

10 A gold snuff box made for the Duc de Choiseul. Though it is only 8 cm wide the paintings on its side and lid show exactly how the Duc's town house in the rue de Richelieu was decorated in the 1750s and how the furniture was arranged.

Scenes from the snuff-box

11 The Duc stands before the fireplace in his reception room. It was still customary for seating furniture to be placed against the walls. Large sofas remained there permanently but chairs were drawn out when needed.

12 The Duc's bedchamber. The bed, sofa, chairs and desk screen are covered in matching floral silk. The cartel clock hangs on a large mirror. Two valets help the Duc to complete his toilet at a dressing table.

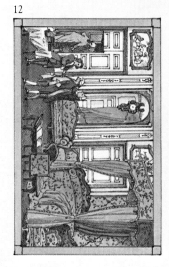

◁ Ground plan of a mid-century Paris town house. For large parties the formal and informal rooms could be used together forming a string of reception rooms for dancing, cards, and conversation. Upstairs were more reception rooms and several more apartments.

13 The Duc holds his *levée* in the state bedchamber. The floor is of polished stucco in various colours. The mirror is topped by a profile of Louis XV in silhouette.

14 The octagonal picture closet. The Duc was a great picture collector. The room is top-lit to leave the walls free for paintings.

15 The Duc confers with his secretaries.

Fashionable interiors

The cost of this decoration was prodigious. 'When a house has been built, nothing is yet accomplished!', a Parisian lamented. 'One has not yet laid out a quarter of the cost; then comes the joiner, the upholsterer, the painter, the gilder, the carver, the cabinet maker and so on.' The cost had to be met, for a person of distinction had to live in Paris, and in style. When the Duc de Choiseul fell from favour and retired to his estate at Chanteloup, it was looked upon as a banishment. Even so, he felt he was obliged to maintain open house there at all times. He had fifty-four servants in the main house and his table was always prepared for up to forty guests, who could hunt deer in his 6,000-acre forest, relax in his fine library or stroll in his large formal garden. He explained that this style of life was not a matter of his personal taste but was obligatory for a man of his position.

The Vincennes porcelain factory was established early in the eighteenth century. Soft-paste porcelain was a European attempt to copy expensive Chinese porcelain. It was not as translucent or as hard as true porcelain, which was first produced at Meissen in Germany in 1709. Though the secret was closely guarded, it was soon being produced at Sèvres and elsewhere.

Furniture and porcelain

1 A marble-topped 'commode' (chest of drawers) with marquetry decoration (a pattern of various coloured veneers) and handles and mounts of ormolu (gilded bronze).

2 Musician's chair in walnut, probably for a cellist. The legs are tucked under to allow a proper positioning of the cellist's feet.

3 Beechwood hair-dressing chair. The hairdresser would attend the lady in her dressing room. The dip in the top of the back enabled her hair to be combed out more conveniently.

4 Beechwood shaving chair. The upper panel is hinged and can be propped in three different positions by a gilded iron support. A fifth leg at the back is splayed out to take the weight of the tilted occupant.

5 Invalid's chair. The hand-cranked mechanism allowed it to be propelled and steered.

6 A writing desk with drawers. On it stands a 'cartonnier' for filing papers.

7 A pair of French flint-lock pistols 1750.

8 A breakfast set of Vincennes soft-paste porcelain for serving hot chocolate.

9 Sèvres tureen in soft-paste porcelain. In 1756 porcelain manufacture was transferred from Vincennes to Sèvres. Louis XV took over the running of the factory and expected all his courtiers to buy its products.

10 One of a pair of perfume burners in onyx with ormolu mounts. Pellets of aromatic paste were burnt within them to perfume a room.

11 A cartel wall clock, so called from the 'cartel' or point at the bottom of the case.

12 Briefcase of Moroccan leather embroidered with silk and gold thread.

13 Gold and enamel spectacle case. Spectacles were no longer clipped onto the nose but had straight side pieces which gripped the temples.

14 A drawing-room dog kennel, gilded and velvet covered, with a down cushion.

15 An undecorated soft-paste porcelain figure, after a painting by Boucher. Such figures were often used as dinner-table decorations.

16-18 and 22-23 (opposite) are based on plates in Diderot's *Encyclopaedia* which was compiled between 1745 and 1772. It was a reference work promoting rationalist thought. Most of the thinkers of the French Enlightenment contributed to it.

16 From the coachmaker. A 'caleche', a light carriage with a folding hood.

17 An upholsterer's workshop, conferring with a client. The upholsterer was a most important tradesman. He provided the elaborate bed hangings, wall coverings, seat upholstery and carpets that were a room's most important components. Upholsterers commissioned other tradesmen – silk mercers, linen drapers, embroiderers, feather dressers and trimmings makers – to make up goods for them. They advised clients on what was fashionable and gradually became entrusted with whole schemes of decoration.

18 Upholsterers at work on the typical Louis XV armchair. Because they were intended to stand against the wall, chairs were frequently not covered at the back. Seats and back rests were padded with horsehair, which was kept in position by techniques borrowed from saddle makers.

19 Silver vessel for cooling wine glasses. They were placed upside down in iced water with their stems resting in the notches of the rim.

16

18 19

20 21

Salons and the Enlightenment

Parisian society was largely presided over by women. It became fashionable for a wife to live in the principal apartment of the house and entertain there, while her husband had a private suite behind the scenes. Elegant Parisian hostesses held *salons* – regular evening entertainments in which people met to exchange ideas in lively conversation. In the most intellectual salons, aristocrats like the Duc de Choiseul mingled with eminent philosophers, scientists and men of letters, such as Voltaire, Montesquieu and Rousseau. In the political and philosophical discussions of the salons the movement known as the Enlightenment was born. It was based upon principles derived from the works of Sir Isaac Newton and the English philosopher John Locke. Its members took nothing on trust; they believed in the spirit of free enquiry, based on observation and governed by reason. This led them to attack many forms of religion, despotism and intolerance and, indirectly, to prepare the way for the French Revolution.

The *Encyclopaedia*

The Enlightenment's optimistic belief that the spread of knowledge would bring happiness to humanity inspired one of its greatest works: the *Encyclopaedia of Sciences, Arts and Industries*, compiled by the writer Denis Diderot. He believed that it was important to study the work of artisans and craftsmen, not just philosophy and the arts. The *Encyclopaedia* provided a comprehensive survey of French manufacturing methods. Diderot's declared aim was to teach artisans to have a better opinion of themselves, philosophers to think along useful lines, and the great to make some worthwhile use of their authority and wealth.

20 Lantern for several candles, suspended by a cord and tassel. The disc above protects the tassel from the heat.
21 A little serving table, with shelves below for plates.
22-24 Coat, waistcoat and breeches. sleeves have become narrow with tight matching cuffs. The waistcoat is getting shorter. Breeches sometimes barely cover the knee-cap.

Jewellery and goldsmith's work
25 Jewelled buckle.
26 Cane top. Canes were still a fashionable accessory
27 Sword pommel. Light swords were still worn by gentlemen until the 1770s. They protruded through the side slits of the waistcoat and the coat.
28 A jewelled decoration for a lady's stomacher.
29-30 Scissors and case.
31 Branched candlestick.
32 Decorated fan-end.
33 The tailor's workshop.

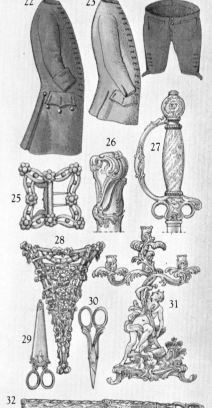

22 23 24

25 26 27

28

29 30 31

32

33

Holkham: a Model Farming Estate

English landowners of the eighteenth century were far more likely than their French counterparts to spend most of the year living in the country on their estates. They had every incentive to increase the value of their land and take an active interest in how it was managed. A growing population meant good prices for their agricultural products. Country matters were also politically important and fashionable. The king himself was known as 'Farmer George' because of the interest he took in his farms at Windsor.

Coke of Holkham

The great wealth of the landowners enabled them to build magnificent country houses, often inspired by buildings they had seen in France and Italy. Houses were surrounded by carefully-planned parkland, which was designed to look like a beautiful and naturally-formed landscape. Thomas Coke, later Earl of Leicester, began work on Holkham Hall in Norfolk in 1734. For thirty years, brick kilns, masons' yards and building debris stood on the north lawn as his creation took shape. It was finally completed in 1762.

Not long afterwards, the vast Holkham estate was inherited by another Thomas Coke, great-nephew of the Earl. Knowing little about farming to begin with, he invited neighbouring farmers to meet him once a year to exchange ideas. These meetings became famous and attracted farming specialists from England and abroad.

Model farms

Agricultural theorists of the eighteenth century urged landowners to use their farms not just for profit but as models to demonstrate new methods. Coke set about establishing a model farming estate at Holkham. The methods he used were not his own inventions; they had been slowly coming into use for the past century. Many were derived from the specialized farming of the Low Countries. But the success of Coke and other progressive landlords was crucial in persuading conservative-minded farmers that there was profit in the 'new-fangled' ideas. Their most important innovation was the growing of new fodder crops – turnips, clover and grasses – which enabled more cattle to be fed through the winter. More cattle meant greater yields of manure and more manure produced heavier crops. The new crops were grown with wheat and barley in a four-year rotation. These and other improvements were possible because more and more farmland was being enclosed, enabling the farmer to grow what he wanted without having to persuade his neighbour to co-operate.

Late-eighteenth-century costume, furniture and objects
1 Woman in a riding coat with deep lapels, and a 'wide awake' hat, also worn by men.
2 After the towering hairstyles of the 1770s the hair and hats of the '80s became extremely broad and less tall.
3 Man in formal coat and breeches and a tricorne hat.
4 A sideboard of 1788 veneered in satinwood with painted decorations.
5 An open knife-case for a sideboard.
6 Flint-glass punch bowl for mixing punch – a hot drink of wine or spirits with milk or water, sugar, lemon and spices.
7 Mahogany dumb waiter with three revolving trays for dishes.
8 A pole fire screen. The height of the shield could be adjusted to protect the face from the heat of the fire.
9 A Pembroke drop-leaved table, for serving breakfast and other informal uses.
10 Pierced silver labels for the necks of wine bottles.
11 A bottle for Holland's geneva, or gin, which was originally made in Holland.
12 A gentleman in informal country clothes of the 1780's.

Early and mid-eighteenth-century furniture from Holkham Hall

13 Marble-topped side table with gilded supports.

14 Table with folding top.

15 Chippendale chair.

16 Armchair by Saunders.

17 Writing desk.

18 A jewelled and enamelled 'hunter' watch of 1780, in its case.

Holkham Hall

19 The south front of Holkham Hall. Holkham was designed by William Kent and begun in 1734. The designs were adapted from Palladio's Villa Mocenego.

20 Cross-section of the main block of Holkham. This part of the house was not intended for everyday living. It housed the grand reception rooms and state bedrooms.

21 From the architect's ground plan of Holkham. Coke and his family had private apartments in the south-east wing. The north-east wing was for guests. Servants' quarters were in the south-west wing. Section A shows the lower floor of the working quarters. There were kitchens, kitchen offices and laundry above, Section B shows the main floor of the reception area.

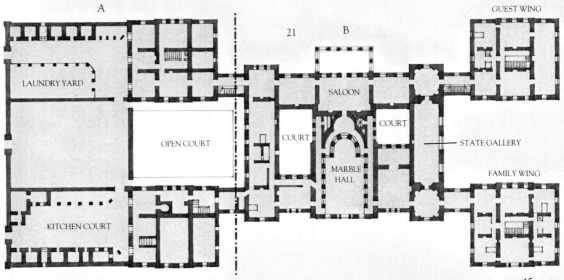

In the long term, the enclosure movement favoured large landowners with more money to invest at the expense of the yeoman farmers with only a few acres. Large proprietors bought up their less successful neighbours until most of the property in an area belonged to one owner, who let it to tenants. Under this arrangement, the landlord provided the basic necessities for good farming: an enclosed convenient farm with decent buildings. The tenant provided the stock, the working capital and his own skills and energy. This new class of tenant farmers tended to be men of some wealth themselves.

New farm buildings

Coke replaced all the old farm buildings at Holkham according to the most advanced agricultural ideas. Barns, stables and cattle houses were ranged round a rectangular courtyard. This reduced the distance between buildings, made cleaning and feeding the animals easier, and allowed manure to drain into a central midden. The large-scale over-wintering of cattle led to the construction of carefully planned cattle houses, with paved standing divisions between the stalls, and fixed food containers. At Holkham the cattle houses had slate plinths which did not rot, and wooden rollers at the front of mangers so that the cows' necks did not wear down the edges.

The new farmhouses at Holkham were so fine that it was said that Coke had provided 'gentlemen's houses' for his tenants. The standard provision was two parlours, a study or business room, four main bedrooms (not including the attics), two kitchens (one a living kitchen for the farm servants), two pantries, a larder and a storeroom. A successful tenant farmer could afford to live like a gentleman. His daughters were well dressed, his sons were sent away to school. In the farmhouse, sofas, pianos and carpets replaced spinning wheels and oak settles. Old beamed kitchens hung with sides of bacon gave way to papered parlours with marble chimney pieces and polished mahogany furniture.

The problems of landless labourers

Farm labourers who possessed no land suffered growing hardship as the century progressed. Population growth increased their numbers faster than the farming industry could absorb them. Many lived in poor one-roomed hovels. Some far-sighted landlords saw the importance of housing workers well. Coke built a village of labourers' cottages, each providing a large living kitchen, a washhouse, scullery and two to four bedrooms. He also built single-storey cottages for the aged and infirm. Cottages for cowmen and those who needed to be near their work were incorporated in the farm layouts.

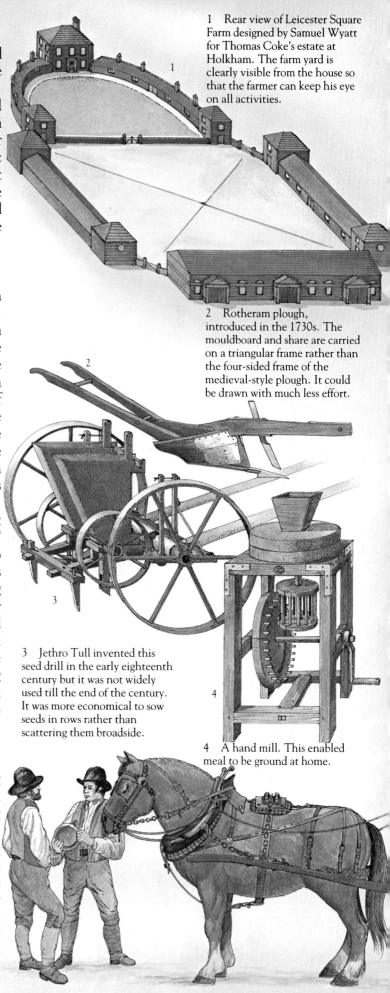

1 Rear view of Leicester Square Farm designed by Samuel Wyatt for Thomas Coke's estate at Holkham. The farm yard is clearly visible from the house so that the farmer can keep his eye on all activities.

2 Rotheram plough, introduced in the 1730s. The mouldboard and share are carried on a triangular frame rather than the four-sided frame of the medieval-style plough. It could be drawn with much less effort.

3 Jethro Tull invented this seed drill in the early eighteenth century but it was not widely used till the end of the century. It was more economical to sow seeds in rows rather than scattering them broadside.

4 A hand mill. This enabled meal to be ground at home.

7 Prosperous tenant farmer at breakfast. There is tea on the table. The chair is protected by a slip cover which was not removed for everyday use.

8 A gout stool for resting painful feet. Gout, said to be caused by drinking too much port, was a comon affliction among the well-to-do.

9 Farm workers with a shire horse drawing an East Anglian box wagon. It has overhanging side boards to increase its loading capacity. Regional variations in design for wagons evolved in the eighteenth century. Larger farms and high yields created a demand for something larger than the farm cart for harvesting. Village craftsmen adapted the heavy carrier's wagon to the needs of their own locality.

10 Register grate. It had an adjustable plate to vary the size of the chimney opening and control the draught.

11 Hob grate. Cast iron panels on either side of the grate supported hobs on which pots and kettles could be heated.

12 Bramah water closet, patented in 1778. The wooden surround is omitted to show the mechanism.

13 A labourer's hovel.

14 Model cottages for labourers. In front of them stands an early nineteenth-century landowner. He is inspecting an improved breed of sheep.

15 Ground plan of the cottages.

5A Wooden rick stand. It is supported on staddle stones to prevent rats reaching the corn.
B Cast iron rick stand.

6 A winnowing machine for separating the outer husks from the grain after threshing.

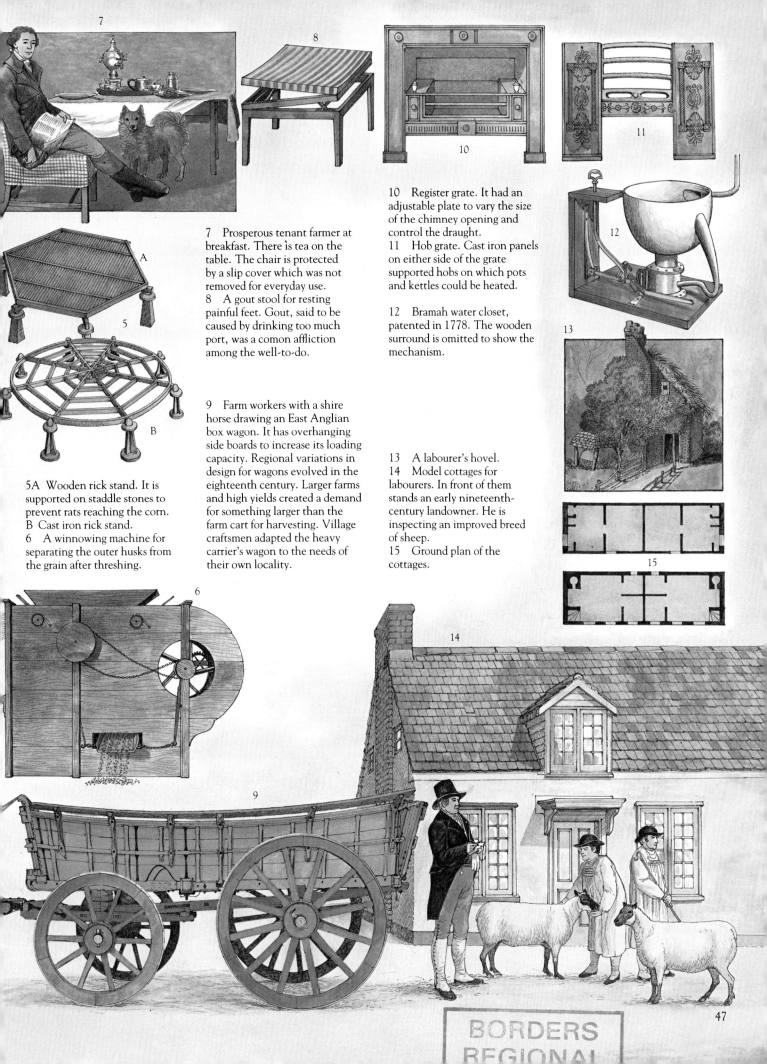

Booklist

GENERAL WORKS *The History of Technology* by C. Singer (Oxford 1956); *The Structures of Everyday Life* [Civilisation and Capitalism Vol. 1] by F. Braudel (Collins 1981); *Authentic Decor, the Domestic Interior 1620–1920* by Peter Thornton (Weidenfeld and Nicholson 1984).

THE MERCHANT OF PRATO *The Merchant of Prato* by Iris Origo (Penguin Books 1963); *A Concise Encyclopaedia of the Italian Renaissance* by J.R. Hale (Thames and Hudson 1981); *Everyday Life in Renaissance Times* by E.R. Chamberlain (Batsford 1965); *The Rise and Fall of the House of Medici* by C. Hibbert (Penguin Books 1979).

THE FIFTEENTH CENTURY MANOR *The Making of the English Landscape* by W.G. Hoskins (Hodder and Stoughton 1955); *Life in the English Country House* by M. Girouard (Yale University Press 1978); *Our Forgotten Past, Seven Centuries of Life on the Land* ed. J. Blum (Thames and Hudson 1982).

NUREMBERG *Nuremberg in the sixteenth century* by G. Strauss (1966); *Nuremberg, a Renaissance city* by J.C. Smith (1983); *Durer and his world* by M. Steck (Thames and Hudson 1964).

EARLY TUDOR ENGLAND *Lavenham, 700 years of textile making* by D. Dymond and A. Betterton; *The Story of the Mary Rose* by E. Bradford (Hamish Hamilton 1982); *European Culture and Overseas Expansion* by C.M. Cipolla (Pelican Books 1970).

SPAIN *Daily Life in Spain in the Golden Age* by M. Desjourneaux (Allen and Unwin 1970); *The Golden Age of Spain 1516–1659* by A.D. Ortiz (Weidenfeld and Nicolson 1971); *The Mediterranean and the Mediterranean World in the age of Philip II* by F. Braudel (Fontana 1975); *The Age of Exploration* by J. Hale (Time Life 1974).

JAMESTOWN *Martin's Hundred* by I.N. Hume (Gollancz 1982); *New Discoveries at Jamestown* by J. Cotter and J.P. Hudson (National Parks Service Washington 1957); *Jamestown, the First English Colony* by M.J. Fishwick (Harper and Row 1965).

EARLY SEVENTEENTH CENTURY FRANCE *Seventeenth Century Interior Decoration in England, France and Holland* by P. Thornton (Yale University Press 1978); *Art and Architecture in France 1500–1700* by A. Blunt (Pelican History of Art 1970); *A Companion to French Studies* by D.G. Charlton (Methuen 1972).

HOLLAND *Daily Life in Rembrandt's Holland* by P. Zuruther (Weidenfeld and Nicolson 1962); *Amsterdam, the Gold Age* by R. Kistemaker and R. van Gelder (Abbeville Press New York 1983); *A History of Dutch Life and Art* by J.J.M. Timmers (Nelson 1959).

NEW ENGLAND *Everyday Life in the Massachusetts Bay Colony* By G. Dow (Benjamin Blom New York 1935); *Everyday Life in Colonial America* (Batsford 1965).

EIGHTEENTH CENTURY FRANCE *Daily Life at Versailles in the 17th and 18th Centuries* by J. Levron (Allen and Unwin 1968); *The Eighteenth Century, Europe in the Age of Enlightenment* by A. Cobban (Thames and Hudson 1969); *A Diderot Pictorial Encyclopaedia of Trades and Industries* (Dover Publications 1959).

REFORMING FARMER *Georgian Model Farms* by J.M. Robinson (Clarendon Press 1983); *The Land* by J. Higgs (Studio Vista 1965); *Farm Tools through the Ages* by M. Partridge (Osprey Publications 1973); *Farm Buildings in England and Wales* by J. Woodforde (Routledge and Kegan Paul 1983).

PRINTED IN BELGIUM BY

INTERNATIONAL BOOK PRODUCTION